AI IN IT

How the Next Five Years Will Redefine Technology

(A Practical 5-Year Roadmap for Data Centers, Cloud, Cybersecurity & End User Services, Based on Insights from Leading Artificial Intelligence Models)

Written By:

Manish Kapoor

&

my LLM Buddies

Date Published: 26th March 2025

Dedication

To my two wonderful kids—your love, patience, and unwavering support mean everything to me. Without you, I wouldn't be where I am today. This book is as much yours as it is mine. Here's to one strong family!

Preface

We are witnessing an extraordinary moment - a time when Artificial Intelligence (AI) is no longer confined to the realm of futuristic imagination but has become an indispensable force reshaping industries in real-time. Every sector is scrambling to adapt, yet nowhere is the promise and complexity of AI more profound than within the heart of modern enterprise: IT infrastructure. Hybrid cloud ecosystems and sophisticated data centers are now producing data at rates previously unimaginable, presenting both tremendous challenges and unprecedented opportunities.

For CIOs, CTOs, IT Directors, Architects, and Engineers, the pivotal question has shifted from "if" AI will influence operations to "how" to effectively leverage its power. Strategic adoption of AI holds the potential to enhance efficiency, fortify security, improve resilience, optimize operational costs, and, ultimately, drive greater business value. However, amidst rapid advancements, deciphering AI's practical uses, navigating the buzz, and setting a clear strategic course can feel overwhelming.

This guide emerged from a novel concept: rather than relying solely on human forecasting, we engaged several advanced AI models available today to directly answer: "What are the most impactful and feasible AI use cases that will revolutionize hybrid cloud and data center operations within the next five years?" The comprehensive collection of 110 detailed use cases presented in this volume synthesizes and expands their collective intelligence, carefully curated for practicality and immediate relevance (approximately spanning 2025 - 2030).

This work is intended neither as purely academic nor theoretical; instead, it serves as a tangible roadmap and source of inspiration for IT leaders and practitioners. It demystifies AI's potential by outlining clear, actionable use cases covering the entire spectrum of IT infrastructure—from monitoring, automation, and security, to cost control, governance, and strategic planning.

Each use case adheres to a structured presentation format, offering:

- **Explanation:** Clear definition and AI enablement of each use case.

- **Implementation Strategy:** Essential steps and considerations for execution.

- **Pain Points Addressed:** Specific operational challenges targeted.

- **Key AI Capability:** Fundamental AI technologies required.

- **Savings/Pros:** Tangible benefits and positive impacts.

- **Cons:** Identifiable challenges, risks, and limitations.

Our ambition is to empower you with a comprehensive array of possibilities, enabling informed decisions tailored to your organization's unique objectives, technological maturity, and strategic aspirations. Although crafted with the assistance of AI, this guide strongly underscores the indispensable role of human judgment, ethical considerations, careful strategic alignment, and thoughtful implementation.

We offer this guide openly to the IT community, aspiring to stimulate discussion, foster experimentation, and accelerate responsible, impactful AI integration within hybrid cloud and data center environments. The future of IT operations is unequivocally AI-driven; let this guide serve as your trusted companion on the transformative journey ahead.

We enthusiastically invite your feedback, insights, and dialogue. As AI continues to advance swiftly, collaborative learning will be vital.

Best Regards,

Manish Kapoor

26th March 2025

Table of Contents

Chapter 1. Introduction - AI as the Catalyst for IT Transformation

1.1 The Inevitable AI Wave in IT Infrastructure

Artificial Intelligence (AI) is no longer confined to research labs or niche applications. It permeates our daily lives and is fundamentally reshaping how businesses operate and compete. Within the realm of Information Technology, particularly the complex world of hybrid cloud and data center infrastructure, AI is transitioning from a buzzword to an essential catalyst for transformation. We are witnessing an explosion of data generated by servers, networks, storage arrays, applications, and cloud services. Simultaneously, the pressure on IT departments to deliver more resilient, secure, performant, and cost-effective services has never been greater. The sheer scale and complexity of modern IT environments are rapidly outpacing traditional human capabilities for management and optimization. This is where AI steps in - not merely as another tool, but as a paradigm shift in how we monitor, manage, secure, and strategize our IT infrastructure. Ignoring this wave is not an option; understanding how to ride it strategically is paramount.

1.2 Complexity and Pressure: The Modern IT Challenge

IT infrastructure leaders today face a confluence of escalating challenges:

- **Hybrid Complexity:** Managing workloads and data distributed across on-premises data centers, multiple public clouds, and edge locations creates significant operational overhead and visibility gaps.

- **Data Deluge:** Monitoring tools generate overwhelming volumes of metrics, logs, and traces, making it difficult to separate critical signals from noise and diagnose issues quickly.

- **Relentless Performance Demands:** Business expectations for application performance, availability, and user experience continue to rise, demanding proactive management and instant response.

- **Sophisticated Security Threats:** Cyberattacks are increasing in frequency and sophistication, requiring advanced detection and response capabilities beyond traditional methods.

- **Cost Optimization Pressures:** Cloud spending requires constant vigilance (FinOps), and data center efficiency (energy, space) remains critical for managing budgets and meeting sustainability goals.

- **Compliance and Governance Burden:** Navigating an increasingly complex web of regulations (privacy, security, financial) demands continuous monitoring and evidence collection.

- **Talent Gaps:** Finding and retaining skilled IT professionals capable of managing these complex environments and leveraging new technologies like AI is a persistent challenge.

Traditional IT management approaches, heavily reliant on manual processes, static thresholds, and siloed tools, are struggling to cope with this new reality. Reactive firefighting consumes valuable resources, hinders innovation, and puts the business at risk.

1.3 Beyond Automation: AI's Transformative Potential

While automation has been a cornerstone of IT improvement for years, AI offers capabilities that go far beyond simple scripting or task execution. It introduces intelligence into the process, enabling systems to:

- **Learn:** Identify normal patterns and behaviors from vast datasets.

- **Predict:** Forecast future events, such as hardware failures, capacity exhaustion, or performance degradation, based on subtle leading indicators.

- **Detect Anomalies:** Recognize deviations from normal patterns that signify potential issues or threats, often far earlier than traditional methods.

- **Correlate:** Understand complex relationships between seemingly unrelated events across different IT domains (network, server, application, cloud) to pinpoint root causes.

- **Optimize:** Recommend or automatically implement actions to improve performance, reduce costs, enhance security, or allocate resources more effectively.

- **Understand Language:** Process and interpret human language in tickets, logs, documents, and user interactions to automate tasks and extract insights.

- **Recommend:** Suggest relevant solutions, knowledge articles, configuration changes, or strategic actions based on context and analysis.

By leveraging these capabilities, AI promises to shift IT operations from a predominantly reactive model to one that is increasingly **proactive, predictive, automated, and intelligent.**

This is not just about efficiency gains; it's about fundamentally transforming IT's ability to support and drive business objectives in a complex digital world.

1.4 Genesis of This Guide: Asking AI About AI

Recognizing the transformative potential and the accompanying confusion surrounding AI in IT, we embarked on a unique approach to create this guide. Instead of relying solely on human experts projecting future trends, we turned to the technology itself. We posed a fundamental question to several of the most advanced AI language models available today:

"What are the most impactful and feasible AI use cases for transforming hybrid cloud and data center operations over the next five years?"

This guide represents a curated, elaborated, and structured compilation of the insights generated by these AI models. We focused their output through a pragmatic filter, prioritizing use cases that are not just technically possible but offer tangible value and are likely implementable within a roughly five-year timeframe (considering 2024 as the starting point, looking towards 2029-2030). It is, in essence, AI's perspective on its own role in the future of IT infrastructure management, refined for practical application.

1.5 Who Should Read This Guide?

This guide is intended for a broad range of IT professionals and leaders who are involved in planning, building, operating, or managing hybrid cloud and data center environments. This includes:

- **Chief Information Officers (CIOs) and IT Executives:** Seeking strategic insights into how AI can drive efficiency, reduce risk, and align IT with business goals.

- **IT Directors and VPs of Infrastructure & Operations:** Looking for practical use cases to improve operational stability, performance, and cost-effectiveness.

- **Cloud Architects and Engineers:** Exploring AI-driven methods for optimizing cloud workloads, managing costs (FinOps), and ensuring security.

- **Data Center Managers and Facilities Engineers:** Interested in AI applications for optimizing power, cooling, and physical security.

- **Network Architects and Engineers:** Seeking AI techniques for improving network performance, reliability, and security.

- **Storage Administrators and Database Administrators (DBAs):** Looking for AI-powered optimization and automation for storage and databases.

- **Security Operations (SecOps) Leaders and Analysts:** Exploring AI for advanced threat detection, vulnerability management, and incident response.

- **IT Service Management (ITSM) and AIOps Professionals:** Interested in leveraging AI for smarter incident management, service desk automation, and enhanced user experience.

- **Compliance and Governance Officers:** Seeking automated solutions for monitoring controls and gathering audit evidence.

- **IT Finance and Strategy Planners:** Looking for data-driven approaches to budgeting, portfolio management, and technology planning.

1.6 Structure and Approach: A Practical Framework

This guide is organized into 11 distinct categories, covering the key domains within hybrid cloud and data center operations and strategy:

1. Monitoring & Observability

2. Compute & Infrastructure Automation

3. Storage & Database Optimization

4. Network Performance & Security

5. Cloud Operations & FinOps

6. Security Operations & Threat Intelligence

7. Incident Management & Resolution (ITSM/MIM)

8. Service Desk & End-User Experience

9. Disaster Recovery & Business Continuity

10. Compliance & Governance

11. IT Strategy & Financial Planning

Within each category, specific, actionable use cases (totaling 110) are presented in a consistent, detailed format:

- **Explanation:** A clear description of the use case and the role AI plays.

- **Implementation Strategy:** Practical guidance on prerequisites, key steps, and integration considerations.

- **Pain Points Addressed:** The specific IT challenges the use case aims to solve.

- **Key AI Capability:** Highlighting the core AI technologies involved (e.g., NLP, Anomaly Detection, Forecasting).

- **Savings/Pros:** Outlining the potential benefits, efficiencies, cost savings, or risk reductions.

- **Cons:** Providing a balanced view by discussing potential challenges, limitations, risks, and prerequisites.

This structured approach allows you to quickly grasp the essence of each use case and evaluate its relevance and feasibility for your own organization.

1.7 Navigating the Use Cases: From Possibility to Reality

The 110 use cases presented here represent a broad spectrum of possibilities. It is crucial *not* to view this guide as a prescriptive checklist or a mandate to implement everything. Instead, consider it a rich menu of options. We encourage you to:

- **Identify Pain Points:** Start by reviewing the "Pain Points Addressed" for each use case and identify those that resonate most strongly with your current operational challenges.

- **Assess Potential Impact:** Consider the "Savings/Pros" and align them with your strategic IT and business objectives. Focus on areas with the highest potential value proposition.

- **Evaluate Feasibility:** Review the "Implementation Strategy" and "Cons" sections honestly. Consider your organization's current data maturity, tool landscape, available skills, budget constraints, and cultural readiness.

- **Prioritize:** Select a small number of high-impact, relatively feasible use cases to explore further or pilot. Quick wins can build momentum and demonstrate value.

- **Start Small, Scale Smart:** Many AI implementations benefit from starting with a focused pilot, learning, refining, and then scaling successful initiatives.

- **Integrate, Don't Isolate:** Look for opportunities where different AI use cases can complement each other (e.g., improved monitoring feeding better incident management). Aim for integrated solutions over point tools where possible.

1.8 A Word of Caution: AI is a Tool, Not Magic

While the potential of AI is immense, successful implementation requires a realistic perspective. Remember:

- **Data is Foundational:** AI models are only as good as the data they are trained on and consume. Data quality, accessibility, and integration are critical prerequisites and often the biggest hurdles.

- **Human Oversight is Essential:** AI can provide powerful insights and automation, but human judgment, domain expertise, and ethical oversight remain indispensable. AI suggestions need validation, and automated actions require careful governance.

- **Skills are Required:** Implementing and managing AI solutions requires new skills within the IT team - data science literacy, AI model management, integration expertise, and the ability to interpret AI outputs.

- **Change Management is Key:** Introducing AI often changes workflows and roles. Effective change management communications, and training are vital for successful adoption.

- **Context Matters:** A use case highly successful in one organization might not be suitable for another due to differences in scale, complexity, culture, or priorities.

- **Ethical Considerations:** Be mindful of privacy implications (especially with user data), potential biases in AI models, and transparency in decision-making.

1.9 Embarking on the Journey

The journey towards an AI-powered IT infrastructure is not about a single destination but a continuous process of learning, experimentation, adaptation, and value creation. The following chapters provide a detailed look at the specific opportunities identified by leading AI models - a practical guide grounded in near-term feasibility. Use it to inform your strategy, spark innovation within your teams, and take confident steps towards harnessing the transformative power of Artificial Intelligence in your hybrid cloud and data center environments. The future of efficient, resilient, secure, and value-driven IT operations awaits.

Chapter 2. Category 1: Monitoring & Observability (Use Cases)

1. Predictive Hardware Failure Detection

- **Explanation:** AI continuously analyzes streams of operational data like temperature readings, voltage fluctuations, disk SMART statistics, and specific error codes logged by servers, storage arrays, or network devices. By learning patterns that typically precede failures (based on historical data), it can predict that a specific disk, fan, or power supply has a high probability of failing within a defined future window (e.g., next 7 days).
- **Implementation Strategy:** Requires setting up robust collection pipelines for hardware telemetry and system logs into a centralized platform (e.g., AIOps tool, data lake). AI models (often time-series analysis or survival analysis) are trained on historical failure data correlated with preceding sensor readings. Alerts generated by the model must integrate into existing monitoring dashboards and ITSM ticketing systems to trigger proactive maintenance workflows (e.g., creating a work order for component replacement).
- **Pain Points Addressed:** Avoids sudden, service-impacting outages caused by hardware dying unexpectedly. Shifts maintenance from a reactive, emergency footing (often costly and disruptive) to a planned, proactive schedule. Reduces the direct and indirect costs associated with system downtime (e.g., lost revenue, productivity).
- **Key AI Capability:** Primarily **Time-Series Forecasting** (predicting future events based on past time-stamped data) and **Anomaly Detection** (identifying unusual deviations in sensor readings that might indicate stress). Potentially **Classification** (classifying a device state as 'likely to fail').
- **Savings/Pros:** Significantly cuts costs associated with unplanned downtime and emergency repairs (Est: 15-25% fewer hardware P1s). Allows scheduling maintenance during off-peak hours, minimizing business disruption. Optimizes spare parts inventory. Increases overall service reliability and user trust.
- **Cons:** Heavily reliant on the availability and quality of detailed historical sensor and failure data for training. Models can generate false positives (predicting failures that don't occur), requiring careful tuning and potentially validation steps. Integrating diverse hardware telemetry sources can be technically complex.

2. Metric Anomaly Detection (Dynamic Thresholding)

- **Explanation:** Standard monitoring uses fixed thresholds (e.g., CPU > 90%), which often trigger false alarms during normal peaks or miss subtle issues below the threshold. AI learns the unique normal operating range for each metric on each system, considering time of day, day of week, or business cycles (e.g., month-end processing). It then alerts only on statistically significant deviations from *this learned baseline*, making alerts more meaningful.

- **Implementation Strategy:** Feed granular performance metrics (CPU, RAM, network, disk I/O, custom application metrics) into an AIOps platform or monitoring tool with AI capabilities. The platform automatically trains models (e.g., variations of ARIMA, clustering, autoencoders) to establish dynamic baselines. Configure alerting rules to trigger based on detected anomalies rather than static thresholds.

- **Pain Points Addressed:** "Alert fatigue" where operators ignore floods of meaningless alerts. Missing early signs of trouble because issues haven't crossed arbitrary static thresholds yet. Wasted effort investigating non-issues.

- **Key AI Capability: Anomaly Detection** (detecting deviations from learned normal patterns), **Pattern Recognition** (identifying recurring normal cycles like daily peaks), **Time-Series Analysis**.

- **Savings/Pros:** Dramatically reduces the number of non-actionable alerts (Est: 60-80% fewer false positives), allowing operations teams to focus on real problems. Enables earlier detection of performance degradation or potential failures. Reduces Mean Time To Detect (MTTD).

- **Cons:** Requires a sufficient period of clean baseline data for accurate learning. Model tuning is necessary to balance sensitivity (catching real issues) and specificity (avoiding false positives). Some highly erratic metrics can be challenging to baseline effectively.

3. Log Pattern Anomaly Detection

- **Explanation:** Modern systems generate massive volumes of text logs. AI algorithms automatically parse these logs, cluster similar messages together (even if slightly different), and learn the normal frequency and sequence of log patterns. It then flags new, unusual error messages, unexpected sequences of events, or significant changes in the frequency of certain log types, which often indicate application bugs, misconfigurations, or security events.

- **Implementation Strategy:** Centralize logs from various sources (systems, applications, security devices) into a log management or AIOps platform. Employ AI techniques like NLP (for understanding semantics), clustering (e.g., DBSCAN, K-Means adapted for logs), and anomaly detection algorithms to analyze the log stream in near real-time. Alert operators or security analysts about detected log anomalies.

- **Pain Points Addressed:** Humans cannot possibly read and correlate all logs; critical error messages or security indicators get lost in the noise. Troubleshooting often involves slow, manual searching and filtering of logs.

- **Key AI Capability: Natural Language Processing (NLP)** (parsing, understanding log text), **Clustering** (grouping similar messages), **Anomaly Detection** (identifying rare or changed patterns).

- **Savings/Pros:** Significantly speeds up troubleshooting by highlighting relevant anomalous log entries (Est: 50-70% faster error pattern identification). Can provide early

warnings of application failures or security incidents that might not trigger metric alerts. Reduces manual log analysis effort.
- **Cons:** Can be computationally intensive, especially with high log volumes. Requires tuning to filter out noise from benign new log patterns (e.g., during software updates). Initial learning phase needs representative data.

4. Cross-Domain Root Cause Analysis Correlation

- **Explanation:** When an application slows down, the cause could be the app code, the database, the server OS, the network, storage, or even a cloud provider issue. AI correlates data (events, logs, metric anomalies, configuration changes) from *all* these domains, understanding their dependencies (often via topology mapping), to identify the sequence of events and pinpoint the most probable originating cause of the incident, rather than just surface symptoms.
- **Implementation Strategy:** Requires an AIOps platform capable of ingesting and integrating data from diverse monitoring tools (APM, Infrastructure Monitoring, Log Management, Network Monitoring, CloudWatch/Azure Monitor etc.). Leverage or build topology maps (CMDB data is key). Use AI algorithms like graph analysis (to trace dependencies), Bayesian networks (for probabilistic reasoning), or advanced correlation engines to connect related events across time and domains. Present the findings as a correlated incident with likely root cause(s).
- **Pain Points Addressed:** Siloed monitoring tools provide narrow views. Incident "war rooms" spend hours manually correlating data from different teams/tools. The true root cause is often obscured by cascading symptoms.
- **Key AI Capability: Graph Analysis** (modeling and analyzing relationships/dependencies), **Correlation Engines** (finding statistical relationships between events/metrics), **Probabilistic Modeling** (calculating likelihood of causes), **Topology Mapping**.
- **Savings/Pros:** Dramatically reduces Mean Time To Resolution (MTTR) by quickly identifying the likely root cause (Est: 30-50% faster RCI). Avoids wasted effort chasing symptoms. Reduces the size and duration of incident war rooms. Improves understanding of complex system interactions.
- **Cons:** Very high implementation complexity, heavily dependent on accurate topology/CMDB data (often a weakness), requires significant data integration effort across potentially disparate tools.

5. Predictive Application Performance Degradation

- **Explanation:** AI analyzes detailed Application Performance Monitoring (APM) data (e.g., transaction traces, response times, error rates) along with underlying infrastructure metrics. It learns the subtle patterns and leading indicators (e.g., increasing garbage collection frequency, slightly rising DB query times) that predict an impending slowdown or failure *before* response times cross critical SLA thresholds or users start complaining.

- **Implementation Strategy:** Feed granular APM data (e.g., from Dynatrace, Datadog, New Relic) and related infrastructure metrics into AI models. Use time-series forecasting or regression techniques to predict future values of key performance indicators (KPIs) like response time or error rate. Configure alerts based on these predictions (e.g., "Predicted response time > 2s in 1 hour") or trigger automated scaling/mitigation actions.
- **Pain Points Addressed:** Application performance issues typically detected only after users are impacted. Reactive scaling leads to poor user experience during ramp-up. Difficulty meeting performance SLAs consistently.
- **Key AI Capability: Time-Series Forecasting** (predicting future metric values), **Regression Analysis** (modeling relationships between predictor metrics and performance outcomes), **Anomaly Detection** (spotting deviations in leading indicators).
- **Savings/Pros:** Enables proactive intervention (scaling, tuning, fixing) to prevent user-visible slowdowns (Est: 20-40% fewer performance complaints). Improves user experience and satisfaction. Helps maintain SLA compliance. Optimizes resource usage by scaling predictively.
- **Cons:** Requires investment in comprehensive APM tooling. Models often need to be tuned specifically for each critical application's behavior. Predictive accuracy depends on the lead time and predictability of the degradation pattern.

6. Smart Alert Prioritization & Contextualization

- **Explanation:** Operations teams receive thousands of alerts daily. AI helps by automatically enriching each alert with business context (Which application is affected? How critical is it? Who owns it? Is it customer-facing?) drawn from the CMDB or tagging. It then uses learned patterns and rules to assign a priority based on potential *impact*, not just technical severity (a critical DB server issue matters more if it supports the main trading platform). It also suppresses noisy or duplicate alerts related to the same underlying problem (often handled by Use Case 7.1).
- **Implementation Strategy:** Centralize alerts from all monitoring sources into an AIOps or event management platform. Ensure integration with a well-maintained CMDB or asset inventory system that includes business context and relationships. Configure AI rules or machine learning models (classification) to assess alert context and potential impact, assigning a calculated priority score. Display alerts ranked by this score.
- **Pain Points Addressed:** Operators overwhelmed by sheer alert volume ("alert fatigue"), leading to missed critical alerts. Inconsistent prioritization based on subjective judgment or just technical severity (e.g., disk full on dev server vs. prod server). Wasted time investigating low-impact issues.
- **Key AI Capability: Classification** (assigning priority levels), **NLP** (understanding alert text), **Rule Engines** (applying contextual logic), **Data Enrichment** (pulling CMDB context), **Risk Scoring**.
- **Savings/Pros:** Ensures operators focus on the most impactful issues first (Est: 90%+ accuracy on high-priority alert identification). Reduces noise and distraction significantly.

Leads to faster response times for critical incidents. Improves alignment of Ops activities with business priorities.

- **Cons:** Highly dependent on the accuracy and completeness of the CMDB or contextual data sources. Defining business impact quantitatively can be challenging. Requires careful rule/model tuning.

7. Automated Topology Discovery & Mapping Validation

- **Explanation:** Maintaining an accurate map of how applications, servers, network devices, and cloud services are interconnected (topology) is vital but difficult manually. AI analyzes network traffic patterns (flows), configuration data (e.g., from routers, load balancers, cloud APIs), and agent data to automatically discover these connections and build a topology map. It can also continuously compare this discovered map against the data in the CMDB, highlighting discrepancies (e.g., undocumented servers, incorrect relationships) for validation.
- **Implementation Strategy:** Deploy network flow collectors, configuration scraping tools, or leverage discovery agents/cloud provider APIs. Feed this data into an AIOps or dedicated Discovery tool. Use AI techniques like graph analysis and pattern recognition to infer connections and build the map. Implement reconciliation logic to compare the discovered map with the existing CMDB data, generating discrepancy reports or triggering update workflows.
- **Pain Points Addressed:** CMDBs are notoriously difficult to keep accurate and up-to-date manually. Inaccurate topology hinders effective impact analysis for changes and incidents. "Shadow IT" or unmanaged assets create security and operational risks.
- **Key AI Capability: Graph Analysis** (representing and analyzing network connections), **Pattern Recognition** (identifying communication patterns), **Data Reconciliation** (comparing discovered data vs. CMDB), **Machine Learning** (inferring connections based on behavior).
- **Savings/Pros:** Provides a much more accurate and current view of the IT environment. Enables reliable impact analysis ("What business services depend on this server?"). Improves accuracy of root cause analysis (Use Case 1.4). Helps identify unmanaged or rogue assets. Reduces manual CMDB maintenance effort (though validation is still needed).
- **Cons:** Network complexity (e.g., NAT, firewalls, overlays) can make accurate discovery challenging. Requires broad network visibility and access to configuration data. Merging discovered data with existing CMDB requires careful rule definition.

8. Business Transaction Monitoring Anomaly Detection

- **Explanation:** This goes beyond simple application response time. AI monitors the end-to-end flow and performance of specific, critical business processes (e.g., "Process New Order," "Complete Stock Trade," "Submit Insurance Claim") as they traverse multiple applications and infrastructure components. It learns the normal duration, throughput, and success rate for these transactions and detects anomalies (e.g., sudden drop in successful orders, slowdown in payment processing step) that directly indicate business impact, even if underlying IT metrics haven't crossed thresholds.

- **Implementation Strategy:** Requires defining and instrumenting key business transactions within APM tools (tagging requests as they flow across services). Feed transaction success/failure data, step timings, and volumes into AI anomaly detection models. Correlate detected business transaction anomalies with underlying IT alerts/metrics to provide business context to IT incidents.
- **Pain Points Addressed:** IT incidents often reported in technical terms with unclear business impact. Difficulty prioritizing IT issues based on actual business harm. Slow reaction to problems affecting revenue or customer experience directly.
- **Key AI Capability: Anomaly Detection** (applied to business KPIs derived from transactions), **Correlation** (linking business anomalies to IT events), **Business Process Mining** (understanding transaction steps).
- **Savings/Pros:** Provides immediate visibility into the business impact of IT issues. Enables explicit prioritization based on business risk (e.g., revenue loss). Facilitates clearer communication between IT and business stakeholders during incidents. Helps meet business-level SLAs.
- **Cons:** Requires significant effort to define and instrument business transactions correctly within applications (developer involvement often needed). Can be complex to correlate accurately across many loosely coupled services.

9. Intelligent Log Summarization for Incidents

- **Explanation:** When an incident occurs, responders often face thousands or millions of log lines from potentially dozens of systems. AI uses Natural Language Processing (NLP) techniques specifically trained on IT logs to automatically read through the relevant logs associated with the incident CIs and timeframe, identify the most salient messages (errors, warnings, critical state changes), and generate a concise, human-readable summary.
- **Implementation Strategy:** Integrate log management platform with ITSM/incident management tool. When an incident is created (or manually triggered), pass the relevant CIs and timeframe to an NLP summarization engine. This engine retrieves logs, filters/ranks messages based on severity and relevance, and uses extractive or abstractive summarization techniques to create the summary. Display the summary directly within the incident ticket.
- **Pain Points Addressed:** Responders waste critical time manually sifting through verbose, noisy logs to understand what happened. Key information can be easily missed. Cognitive overload during high-pressure incidents.
- **Key AI Capability: Natural Language Processing (NLP)** (specifically Summarization, Keyword Extraction, Text Classification adapted for log formats).
- **Savings/Pros:** Dramatically reduces the time needed to understand the sequence of events from logs (Est: 60-80% reduction in analysis time per incident). Allows responders

to grasp the situation faster and start troubleshooting sooner. Reduces errors from missed log messages. Improves consistency in initial diagnosis.

- **Cons:** Summaries might occasionally miss subtle but crucial details or context. Accuracy depends heavily on the quality of the NLP model and its training on relevant log types. Generated summaries still require human interpretation.

10. Predictive Capacity Exhaustion (Compute, Storage, Network)

- **Explanation:** AI analyzes historical utilization trends (e.g., daily/weekly/monthly growth patterns, seasonality) for key infrastructure resources like CPU, RAM, disk space on specific volumes/servers, or network bandwidth on key links. It uses forecasting models to predict when utilization is likely to hit predefined thresholds (e.g., 90% full) based on current trends, providing advance warning (e.g., 30, 60, 90 days out).
- **Implementation Strategy:** Collect and store long-term historical utilization metrics for relevant resources in a monitoring or AIOps platform. Apply appropriate time-series forecasting algorithms (e.g., ARIMA, Prophet, LSTM) considering trends and seasonality. Generate regular capacity forecast reports and trigger alerts when predicted exhaustion dates fall within critical lead times required for procurement or provisioning.
- **Pain Points Addressed:** Running out of critical resources unexpectedly, causing outages or severe performance degradation. Scrambling for emergency procurement at premium prices. Inefficient resource planning based on guesswork.
- **Key AI Capability: Time-Series Forecasting** (predicting future utilization values based on historical patterns).
- **Savings/Pros:** Enables proactive, planned capacity upgrades or resource allocation, avoiding service disruptions (Est: 95%+ accuracy in short-term forecasts). Allows for budget planning well in advance. Optimizes resource utilization by avoiding excessive over-provisioning "just in case." Reduces costs associated with emergency purchases.
- **Cons:** Accuracy depends on the stability and predictability of growth patterns (sudden, unexpected demand spikes are hard to predict). Requires sufficient clean historical data for reliable forecasting. Forecasts need periodic review and adjustment as underlying conditions change.

Chapter 3. Category 2: Compute & Infrastructure Automation (Use Cases)

11. Predictive VM/Container Rightsizing Recommendations

- **Explanation:** Cloud and virtualized environments make it easy to provision resources, but often VMs or containers are allocated more CPU or RAM than they consistently need ("over-provisioning," wasting money) or too little ("under-provisioning," risking performance issues). AI analyzes historical utilization metrics (CPU usage peaks and averages, memory consumption) over a representative period, compares it to the allocated resources, and recommends optimal sizing adjustments (e.g., "Change VM size from Large to Medium," "Increase container memory limit from 1GB to 1.5GB").
- **Implementation Strategy:** Ingest granular utilization metrics (e.g., 5-minute intervals) from cloud provider APIs (CloudWatch, Azure Monitor) or hypervisor tools (vCenter) into a cost optimization or AIOps platform. AI algorithms (regression, classification, or vendor-specific logic) model resource needs based on past usage, factoring in headroom for peaks. Generate regular reports with specific, actionable downsizing/upsizing recommendations, often including estimated cost savings or performance benefits. High-maturity implementations might automate the resizing action after approval.
- **Pain Points Addressed:** Wasted cloud spend due to oversized resources. Performance throttling or application instability due to undersized resources. Manual effort required to analyze utilization and determine appropriate sizes.
- **Key AI Capability: Regression** (predicting needed resources based on usage), **Classification** (categorizing workloads for sizing profiles), **Optimization** (balancing cost vs. performance headroom).
- **Savings/Pros:** Significant direct cost savings on cloud compute bills (Est: 15-30%) by eliminating waste. Improved application performance and stability by addressing under-provisioning. More efficient use of underlying hardware in private clouds. Data-driven capacity management.
- **Cons:** Recommendations need careful validation, as short-term peaks or specific application requirements (e.g., memory-hungry startup) might not be fully captured by average/percentile utilization. Automating resizing actions carries risk if not thoroughly tested. Requires reliable, granular utilization data.

12. AI-Driven Infrastructure Provisioning (Intent-Based)

- **Explanation:** This moves beyond traditional Infrastructure as Code (IaC) where users define *how* to build infrastructure. Here, users declare the *desired outcome* or "intent" (e.g., "Deploy a highly available web application stack meeting PCI compliance, capable of handling 1000 requests/sec"). AI interprets this intent, considers available resources (cloud vs. on-prem), policies (security, cost), and performance requirements, then determines the optimal infrastructure configuration (VM sizes, network rules, load balancers, DB choices) and orchestrates the deployment using underlying IaC tools.

- **Implementation Strategy:** Requires developing or adopting an "Intent Engine" platform. This involves creating models that map high-level intents to specific infrastructure components and configurations. AI uses planning algorithms, optimization techniques, and potentially reinforcement learning (learning from past deployment successes/failures) to generate the deployment plan. Tight integration with cloud APIs, hypervisors, and IaC tools (Terraform, Pulumi, Ansible) is essential for execution. NLP might be used for interpreting natural language intent requests.

- **Pain Points Addressed:** Traditional infrastructure provisioning (even with IaC) requires deep technical expertise, is often slow, complex, and prone to human error, especially in hybrid environments. Ensuring compliance and optimal configuration manually is challenging.

- **Key AI Capability: Planning** (determining steps to achieve a goal), **Optimization** (selecting best resources/configs), **Reinforcement Learning** (improving deployment strategies over time), **Natural Language Understanding** (interpreting intent), **Policy Engines**.

- **Savings/Pros:** Dramatically accelerates application deployment times (Est: 50-70% faster provisioning). Increases consistency and reduces errors by automating complex decision-making. Enforces compliance and best practices automatically. Abstracts infrastructure complexity from developers or application teams.

- **Cons:** Very high implementation complexity and potentially high cost for sophisticated platforms. Requires extremely well-defined service catalogs, policies, and resource metadata. Defining and interpreting "intent" accurately is non-trivial. Less direct control for infrastructure engineers.

13. Automated Configuration Drift Detection & Remediation

- **Explanation:** "Configuration drift" occurs when the actual configuration of a server, network device, or cloud service deviates from its intended, approved state (often defined in IaC templates or compliance baselines). This drift can introduce security risks or instability. AI continuously monitors configurations, compares them against the desired state, automatically flags any discrepancies, and can optionally trigger automated remediation actions (e.g., re-applying the correct configuration via Ansible or Chef).

- **Implementation Strategy:** Establish a "source of truth" for desired configurations (e.g., Git repository with IaC code, compliance policy definitions). Implement tools that continuously scan or receive configuration state data from endpoints, devices, and cloud APIs. Use AI-powered policy engines or pattern matching algorithms to compare actual vs. desired state. Integrate findings with alerting systems and optionally with configuration management tools (Ansible, Puppet, Chef, SaltStack) or cloud automation services to trigger remediation workflows.

- **Pain Points Addressed:** Manual configuration changes bypassing standard processes. Inconsistencies between environments (dev, test, prod). Security vulnerabilities or compliance failures introduced by incorrect settings. Instability caused by unexpected configuration changes.
- **Key AI Capability: Pattern Recognition** (comparing configurations), **Policy Engines** (evaluating compliance rules), **Workflow Automation** (triggering remediation).
- **Savings/Pros:** Greatly improved infrastructure stability and reliability (Est: 90%+ automated detection/remediation rate for defined drifts). Enhanced security posture by quickly correcting unauthorized or insecure changes. Continuous assurance of compliance with internal standards or external regulations. Reduced manual auditing and firefighting.
- **Cons:** Requires a disciplined approach to defining and maintaining the desired state configurations. Automated remediation carries significant risk if not carefully designed and tested - could cause outages if it reverts a necessary emergency change or applies a faulty configuration. Requires broad configuration visibility.

14. Predictive Hardware Maintenance Scheduling

- **Explanation:** This builds upon predictive failure detection (1.1). Once AI predicts a high likelihood of hardware failure, this use case focuses on *optimizing the timing* of the maintenance. It considers the failure prediction window, business impact windows (e.g., avoid peak trading hours), technician availability and location, spare part logistics, and potentially dependencies (e.g., need to migrate workloads first). AI recommends the optimal maintenance slot that minimizes disruption and cost while addressing the predicted failure proactively.
- **Implementation Strategy:** Requires integrating failure predictions (from Use Case 1.1 or similar) with multiple scheduling systems and data sources: business calendars, change management schedules, technician dispatch systems, parts inventory/logistics. Use optimization algorithms (e.g., constraint programming, scheduling algorithms) to find the best time slots that satisfy all constraints (predicted failure window, business constraints, resource availability). Integrate recommendations into maintenance planning tools or work order systems.
- **Pain Points Addressed:** Maintenance performed reactively after failure. Scheduled maintenance causing disruption because it conflicts with critical business periods. Inefficient use of field technicians or maintenance resources. Delays due to parts availability.
- **Key AI Capability: Optimization** (finding the best schedule under constraints), **Scheduling Algorithms**, **Data Integration**.
- **Savings/Pros:** Minimizes business disruption caused by both failures and maintenance activities (Est: 20-30% less emergency maintenance). Improves efficiency of maintenance staff and spare parts logistics. Reduces costs associated with expedited

repairs or overtime. Extends useful hardware life where appropriate by performing timely preventative maintenance.
- **Cons:** Requires complex integration across multiple operational and business systems. Accuracy depends on reliable failure predictions and accurate scheduling data. Balancing proactive maintenance against potential disruption requires careful policy definition.

15. Risk-Based Automated OS Patching Rollout

- **Explanation:** Traditional patching often follows rigid schedules or prioritizes based solely on vendor severity/CVSS score. AI enables a more intelligent approach by calculating a contextualized risk score for each patch on each system. It considers: the severity of the vulnerability (CVSS), whether exploits exist in the wild (threat intelligence), the criticality of the asset (from CMDB), the system's exposure (e.g., internet-facing?), and potentially results from automated testing or pilot deployments. Based on this risk score, AI orchestrates a phased rollout, prioritizing high-risk/high-impact systems first while potentially delaying lower-risk patches or implementing them more slowly.
- **Implementation Strategy:** Integrate patching tools with vulnerability scanners, CMDB, threat intelligence feeds, and potentially automated testing frameworks. Develop an AI risk scoring model that weighs these different factors according to organizational policy. Configure the automated patching system (e.g., SCCM, BigFix, Ansible) to execute patching waves based on the AI-driven prioritization and rollout plan. Monitor deployment success and feedback into the risk model.
- **Pain Points Addressed:** Slow patching cycles leaving critical vulnerabilities exposed for too long. Patching causing unexpected outages due to unforeseen conflicts or bugs. Difficulty focusing limited patching resources on the most critical risks first. "Patch Tuesday" overload.
- **Key AI Capability: Risk Scoring Models**, **Classification** (prioritizing assets/patches), **Orchestration** (controlling patching tools), **Threat Intelligence Correlation**.
- **Savings/Pros:** Significantly accelerates the deployment of truly critical security patches (Est: 30-50% faster for highest risk), measurably reducing the window of exposure. Reduces the risk of patch-induced outages through more targeted rollouts and potentially pre-testing insights. Improves overall security compliance posture. Optimizes use of maintenance windows and patching team effort.
- **Cons:** High implementation complexity, involving integration of multiple security and operations tools. Success depends heavily on the accuracy of input data (vuln scans, CMDB, threat intel). Risk of automated rollout causing widespread issues if the risk assessment or patch applicability logic is flawed requires very careful validation and phased implementation.

16. Workload Placement Optimization (Private Cloud/DC)

- **Explanation:** In a private cloud or virtualized data center, AI helps decide which physical host is the best place to run a given virtual machine (VM) or container. It analyzes the workload's resource needs (CPU, RAM, network I/O, disk I/O patterns) and the current utilization and capabilities of available hosts, considering factors like resource contention ("noisy neighbors"), power consumption, affinity rules (e.g., keep DB and App servers close), anti-affinity rules (e.g., don't run redundant app servers on the same host), and license constraints (e.g., pinning Oracle VMs to specific licensed hosts). The goal is to balance load, maximize hardware utilization, ensure performance, and adhere to placement constraints.
- **Implementation Strategy:** Requires tools to profile workload resource consumption patterns and monitor host utilization and capabilities in real-time. Integrate with the hypervisor's management platform (e.g., vCenter DRS, OpenStack Nova Scheduler). Use AI optimization algorithms (like bin packing variations, constraint satisfaction solvers, or potentially reinforcement learning) to continuously evaluate and recommend or automate VM placement/migration decisions.
- **Pain Points Addressed:** Uneven resource utilization across hosts (some overloaded, some idle). Performance issues caused by resource contention between demanding VMs on the same host ("noisy neighbor" problem). Manual effort required for initial VM placement and load balancing. Violations of licensing or HA placement rules.
- **Key AI Capability: Optimization** (maximizing utilization under constraints), **Simulation** (predicting impact of placements), **Constraint Programming** (handling placement rules), **Workload Profiling**.
- **Savings/Pros:** Improved overall hardware utilization (Est: 10-20%), leading to better ROI on infrastructure and potentially deferred hardware purchases. More consistent and predictable application performance due to reduced contention. Automated adherence to placement policies and license constraints. Reduced operational effort for manual load balancing.
- **Cons:** Requires accurate and continuous workload profiling, which can be challenging for bursty apps. Optimization algorithms can be computationally intensive for very large environments. Frequent automated VM migrations (vMotion) can sometimes introduce minor performance overhead or network impact.

17. Predictive Auto-Scaling Based on Application Demand Forecasts

- **Explanation:** Standard cloud auto-scaling reacts to current load (e.g., scale up when CPU > 70%). Predictive auto-scaling uses AI to forecast *upcoming* demand based on historical patterns (time of day, day of week), known events (e.g., marketing campaigns, holidays), or even external factors (e.g., weather impacting e-commerce). It then proactively adds or removes instances *before* the demand change occurs, ensuring resources are ready when needed and removed promptly when not, optimizing both performance and cost.

- **Implementation Strategy:** Collect historical metrics related to application load (e.g., request counts, active users, transaction volume) and corresponding resource utilization. Use time-series forecasting models to predict future load. Integrate these predictions with the cloud provider's auto-scaling mechanisms (e.g., through custom metrics or APIs) to trigger scaling events based on forecast values rather than just current metrics.
- **Pain Points Addressed:** Reactive scaling results in delays provisioning new instances during sudden load increases, causing poor performance or errors. Keeping excess capacity provisioned "just in case" during idle periods wastes money. Scaling based purely on CPU/memory can miss application-specific bottlenecks.
- **Key AI Capability: Time-Series Forecasting** (predicting future load/demand).
- **Savings/Pros:** Smoother application performance during load fluctuations by having capacity ready in advance. Reduced costs (Est: 10-25% vs. reactive) by de-provisioning idle resources more quickly based on predicted lulls. More efficient resource utilization overall. Can potentially use cheaper spot instances more reliably if scaling actions are predictive.
- **Cons:** Predictive accuracy is limited for truly unpredictable, sudden demand spikes. Requires reliable historical load data and identifiable patterns. May require custom integration work with cloud provider auto-scaling services. Needs careful tuning to avoid scaling unnecessarily based on inaccurate forecasts.

18. Automated Bare-Metal Provisioning Optimization

- **Explanation:** Provisioning physical ("bare-metal") servers involves a sequence of time-consuming steps: firmware updates, BIOS configuration, network boot (PXE), OS installation, configuration management agent install, etc. AI can optimize this workflow by analyzing historical task durations, predicting potential bottlenecks (e.g., network contention during image downloads), and potentially parallelizing non-dependent tasks safely across multiple servers being provisioned simultaneously.
- **Implementation Strategy:** Requires a bare-metal provisioning tool (like MAAS, Ironic, Cobbler, or vendor-specific tools) that logs detailed task timings. Analyze this historical data to model task durations and dependencies. Use workflow optimization algorithms or potentially simulation to identify the optimal sequence and potential for parallel execution. Integrate the optimized workflow back into the provisioning tool's orchestration engine.
- **Pain Points Addressed:** Provisioning physical servers is often a slow, manual, and error-prone process compared to VMs or cloud instances. Delays in getting hardware ready impact project timelines. Inconsistencies in configuration can occur.
- **Key AI Capability: Workflow Optimization, Scheduling Algorithms, Process Mining** (analyzing past workflows).
- **Savings/Pros:** Significantly reduces the time required to get new physical servers operational (Est: 40-60% faster). Increases consistency and reduces configuration errors. Allows infrastructure teams to respond faster to demands requiring physical hardware (e.g., for specific performance needs, legacy apps, or virtualization hosts).

- **Cons:** Primarily applicable to organizations that still manage a significant number of physical servers directly. Requires integration with specific bare-metal provisioning tools. Optimization gains depend on the nature of the provisioning tasks and potential for parallelization.

19. Software License Optimization Based on Usage Analysis

- **Explanation:** Organizations often overspend on software licenses because they buy more than needed or fail to track actual usage. AI analyzes data from license management servers, application login/usage logs, or endpoint agents to identify licenses that are assigned but rarely or never used, or instances where users have multiple licenses for similar products. It provides reports recommending license reclamation ("harvesting") or potential shifts to different license types (e.g., concurrent vs. named user) for cost savings.
- **Implementation Strategy:** Integrate data sources that track software installation and usage (license servers like FlexLM, application-specific logs, endpoint inventory/usage tools like SCCM/Intune). Use AI/analytics tools to compare entitlement data (what you own) with actual usage data. Identify patterns of underutilization, non-usage, or redundant installations. Generate actionable reports for software asset managers (SAM) or trigger automated reclamation workflows where feasible.
- **Pain Points Addressed:** Significant wastage on expensive software licenses ("shelfware"). Non-compliance risk from using un-licensed software or exceeding license counts. Difficulty manually tracking usage across thousands of users and devices. Complex license models make optimization hard.
- **Key AI Capability: Usage Pattern Analysis, Anomaly Detection** (identifying zero usage), **Data Integration and Reconciliation**.
- **Savings/Pros:** Direct and often substantial software license cost savings (Est: 10-20%) through reclamation and right-sizing. Improved license compliance and reduced audit risk. Better data for negotiating future vendor contracts. Frees up licenses for users who actually need them.
- **Cons:** Requires reliable mechanisms for tracking software usage, which can be challenging for some applications or license models. Interpreting complex license agreements (e.g., core-based, indirect access) often still requires human expertise. Automated reclamation needs careful handling to avoid disrupting users.

20. Self-Healing Infrastructure (Automated VM/Container Recycling)

- **Explanation:** When AI monitoring (like Use Cases 1.2, 1.3, 1.5) detects a known failure pattern or unrecoverable state in a VM or container (e.g., application consistently unresponsive, critical process crashed, out of memory errors persisting), it can automatically trigger a "self-healing" action. This typically involves gracefully restarting the service, recycling the container instance, or even terminating the unhealthy VM and spinning up a new one from a known good image, restoring service without human intervention for common, predefined issues.

- **Implementation Strategy:** Define specific failure signatures (patterns of metrics, logs, or health checks) that warrant automated remediation. Develop corresponding automated recovery scripts or playbooks (e.g., restart service, kill pod, reboot VM, terminate/replace instance). Use an AIOps or automation platform to trigger the correct playbook when AI monitoring detects a matching failure signature. Ensure actions are logged and alerts are potentially suppressed if recovery is successful.

- **Pain Points Addressed:** Operations staff spend significant time performing repetitive manual recovery actions (restarting services, rebooting servers). Minor issues can impact application availability until manually addressed. Inconsistent responses to common failures.

- **Key AI Capability: Anomaly Detection / Pattern Recognition** (identifying the failure state), **Workflow Automation** (triggering the remediation action), **Rule Engines** (mapping signatures to actions).

- **Savings/Pros:** Significantly improves application availability and reduces MTTR for common, known failures (Est: 70-90% automated recovery). Reduces operational toil and frees up human operators for more complex issues. Ensures consistent and rapid response 24/7.

- **Cons:** Carries significant risk if not implemented carefully. Incorrectly identifying a failure state or applying the wrong remediation could worsen an outage or cause data loss. Requires thorough testing and validation of failure signatures and recovery playbooks. Should initially be implemented with human approval or for non-critical systems. Need mechanisms to prevent endless restart loops.

Chapter 4. Category 3: Storage & Database Optimization (Use Cases)

21. AI-Recommended Database Index Creation/Removal

- **Explanation:** Database performance heavily relies on having the right indexes, but determining these manually is complex. AI analyzes actual database query workloads, focusing on slow-running queries or frequently executed ones. It examines their execution plans (how the database retrieves data) and simulates the potential performance impact (positive or negative) of adding specific indexes or removing existing ones that are unused, infrequently used, or redundant. It then presents these recommendations, often with estimated performance gains or storage savings, to Database Administrators (DBAs).
- **Implementation Strategy:** Requires integration with the database to capture query execution plans, workload statistics (query frequency, duration), and schema information. AI platforms or specialized database monitoring tools ingest this data. They use cost-based simulation models (mimicking the database optimizer) or machine learning trained on past index changes to evaluate potential indexes. Recommendations are typically presented in a dashboard or report for DBA review and action.
- **Pain Points Addressed:** Slow application performance caused by inefficient database queries. The complexity and time required for DBAs to manually analyze workloads and tune indexes effectively. Wasted storage space and potential negative performance impact from unused or poorly designed indexes.
- **Key AI Capability: Query Plan Analysis, Simulation** (cost-based modeling), **Optimization** (finding best index set), potentially **Machine Learning** (learning from past tuning).
- **Savings/Pros:** Significant improvement in application response times dependent on database queries (Est: 20-40% faster problem queries). Reduced load on the database server (CPU, I/O). Frees up valuable DBA time from routine index tuning to focus on higher-level tasks. Optimizes storage consumption.
- **Cons:** Recommendations absolutely require expert DBA validation before implementation, as AI might miss application-specific context or edge cases, and incorrect indexes can severely harm performance. Effectiveness depends on the quality and representativeness of the analyzed query workload.

22. Predictive Storage Tiering Automation

- **Explanation:** Storing all data on expensive, high-performance storage (like SSDs) is often cost-prohibitive. Storage tiering aims to place frequently accessed ("hot") data on fast tiers and less frequently accessed ("cold") data on cheaper, slower tiers (like HDDs or cloud object storage). AI predicts the future access probability of data blocks or files based on historical access patterns (recency, frequency, application context) and automatically migrates data between tiers according to defined policies, optimizing both performance and cost dynamically.

- **Implementation Strategy:** Requires storage systems or software-defined storage solutions that support automated tiering and provide APIs for control. AI monitors data access patterns at a granular level. It uses classification algorithms (to categorize data as hot/warm/cold based on access) and potentially forecasting (to predict future access likelihood). Based on policy rules (e.g., "Keep data accessed in last 30 days on Tier 1"), the AI engine instructs the storage system to move data blocks/files between tiers.
- **Pain Points Addressed:** High cost of storing large volumes of inactive data on expensive primary storage. Manual tiering processes are slow, inefficient, and often reactive. Performance issues when frequently accessed data resides on slow tiers.
- **Key AI Capability: Classification** (hot/warm/cold data), **Forecasting** (predicting future access), **Policy Enforcement Automation**.
- **Savings/Pros:** Significant reduction in overall storage costs (Est: 15-30%) by utilizing cheaper tiers effectively. Ensures frequently accessed data resides on high-performance tiers, optimizing application performance. Fully automated operation reduces manual effort.
- **Cons:** Requires storage infrastructure that supports automated, policy-driven tiering. Incorrect predictions or overly aggressive tiering could lead to performance degradation if data needed quickly has been moved to a slow tier (requiring retrieval time). Defining appropriate policies is crucial.

23. Database Performance Anomaly Detection

- **Explanation:** This goes deeper than standard database health monitoring. AI analyzes fine-grained database-internal performance metrics that often indicate subtle problems - things like specific wait events (e.g., latch free, log file sync), lock contention durations, buffer cache hit ratio degradation, unusual changes in query execution plans, or sudden increases in specific error types. By learning the normal baseline for these metrics under different workload conditions, AI can detect anomalies that often precede major performance degradation or point towards inefficient code, configuration issues, or even security probing.
- **Implementation Strategy:** Deploy database monitoring tools capable of collecting deep, internal performance metrics (often requiring specific agents or database permissions). Feed this granular telemetry into an AIOps or specialized database monitoring platform with AI capabilities. AI establishes dynamic baselines for these complex metrics and alerts DBAs when significant, statistically relevant deviations occur, often providing context like associated queries or sessions.
- **Pain Points Addressed:** Database performance issues that build gradually and are missed by high-level monitoring until they cause major impact. Intermittent problems

that are hard to diagnose reactively. Difficulty distinguishing normal fluctuations from real issues in complex metrics.

- **Key AI Capability: Anomaly Detection** (applied to specialized DB metrics), **Correlation** (linking anomalies to specific queries/sessions), **Pattern Recognition.**
- **Savings/Pros:** Enables early detection and proactive tuning of developing database bottlenecks *before* they significantly impact applications. Faster diagnosis of intermittent or complex performance issues. Can sometimes detect security anomalies like unusual query patterns. Optimizes resource usage within the database.
- **Cons:** Can generate noise if baselines are not properly learned or if the environment is inherently very volatile. Requires specialized database monitoring tools and expertise to interpret the findings. Accessing deep metrics might have a slight performance overhead on the database itself.

24. Automated Backup Policy Optimization & Validation

- **Explanation:** AI analyzes factors like data change rates for different datasets, business-defined Recovery Point Objectives (RPO - max acceptable data loss) and Recovery Time Objectives (RTO - max acceptable downtime), compliance requirements, backup window constraints, and network/storage performance. Based on this, it recommends optimal backup schedules (frequency, timing), methods (full vs. incremental vs. differential), and potentially retention policies to meet objectives efficiently. Additionally, AI can automate parts of backup validation by triggering test restores, performing checksum comparisons, or mounting backups to check file system integrity, providing assurance beyond simple "job completed successfully" status.
- **Implementation Strategy:** Integrate AI platform with backup software APIs, storage systems, and potentially CMDB (for RPO/RTO requirements). Analyze historical backup job logs, data change rate information from servers/databases, and infrastructure performance data. Use AI optimization algorithms to find schedules balancing RPO/RTO, cost, and resource usage. Implement automated validation scripts triggered post-backup or periodically, feeding results back into the monitoring/reporting system.
- **Pain Points Addressed:** Inefficient backup schedules consuming excessive network bandwidth or storage. Uncertainty whether RPO targets are actually being met. Backup jobs failing silently or backups being corrupt but unnoticed until a restore is needed. Manual validation is time-consuming and often skipped.
- **Key AI Capability: Optimization** (scheduling, policy selection), **Pattern Recognition** (change rates), **Automation** (validation checks), **Constraint Programming.**
- **Savings/Pros:** Improved confidence in meeting RPO/RTO targets. Potential reduction in backup storage consumption and network traffic during backup windows (Est: 10-20%). Increased reliability of data recovery. Reduced manual effort in managing schedules and validating backups. Supports audit requirements for demonstrating recoverability.

- **Cons:** Defining complex RPO/RTO requirements across many applications requires careful modeling. Automated validation needs robust scripting and can consume extra resources (for test restores). Optimizing across multiple backup tools can be complex.

25. Storage Performance Bottleneck Prediction/Identification

- **Explanation:** When applications depending on shared storage (like a SAN or NAS) experience slowdowns, pinpointing the cause is often difficult (Is it the host HBA? The SAN switch? The storage array LUN/controller?). AI correlates performance metrics collected from all components along the I/O path - host server (disk queue length), hypervisor (storage latency), SAN fabric switches (port utilization, errors), and the storage array itself (LUN latency, controller CPU, cache hit rate). By analyzing these correlated metrics over time, AI can predict developing bottlenecks or rapidly identify the component most likely responsible for an existing latency issue.
- **Implementation Strategy:** Requires deploying monitoring agents or utilizing APIs to collect performance metrics from servers, hypervisors, SAN switches (via SNMP or specific APIs), and storage arrays (vendor-specific APIs or standards like SMI-S). Feed this end-to-end data into an AIOps or specialized storage monitoring platform. Use AI correlation and forecasting techniques to identify relationships and highlight bottleneck points (e.g., "High latency on LUN X correlates with high controller CPU on Array Y").
- **Pain Points Addressed:** Difficulty troubleshooting intermittent or complex storage performance issues. "Finger-pointing" between server, network, and storage teams. Slow resolution times for storage-related application slowdowns.
- **Key AI Capability: Correlation** (across multiple infrastructure layers), **Forecasting** (predicting latency spikes), **Root Cause Analysis** (pinpointing bottleneck component).
- **Savings/Pros:** Significantly faster identification and resolution of storage performance bottlenecks (Est: 30-50% faster identification). Enables targeted optimization efforts (e.g., tuning array, moving workload, upgrading specific component). Reduces application impact from storage slowdowns. Improves collaboration between teams by providing data-driven evidence.
- **Cons:** Requires integration with potentially multiple, often proprietary, monitoring interfaces across different vendor equipment. Mapping the complete I/O path accurately can be challenging in complex SANs. Interpreting correlated data still often requires storage expertise.

26. IOPS & Throughput Prediction for Workload Migration/Placement

- **Explanation:** When migrating an application to a new storage system (e.g., different array model, cloud storage tier, hyperconverged infrastructure) or placing a new workload, accurately predicting its storage performance needs (IOPS, throughput/MBps, latency sensitivity) is crucial. AI analyzes the historical I/O behavior of the workload in its source environment (peak/average IOPS, read/write ratios, block size distribution) and uses this profile, potentially combined with benchmarks of the target storage platform, to predict the required performance characteristics and recommend appropriate target storage configuration or tier.

- **Implementation Strategy:** Requires tools capable of profiling application I/O patterns at the source (VM/server level). Ingest this profiling data along with specifications or benchmark results for target storage options. Use AI models (regression, simulation, or classification based on workload types) to predict the performance needs and match them to suitable target storage capabilities. Provide sizing recommendations (e.g., specific cloud disk type/size, required array cache) as part of migration planning.
- **Pain Points Addressed:** Migrating applications only to find the new storage cannot handle the performance demands, requiring costly rework. Over-provisioning expensive storage performance "just in case." Unpredictable performance ("noisy neighbor") issues after consolidating workloads onto new storage.
- **Key AI Capability: Workload Characterization/Profiling**, **Regression** (predicting target needs), **Simulation** (modeling performance on target), **Benchmarking Analysis**.
- **Savings/Pros:** Enables accurate "right-sizing" of storage performance during migrations or new deployments, balancing cost and performance effectively. Reduces the risk of performance issues post-migration. Avoids wasted spend on unnecessary performance headroom. Leads to more predictable performance in consolidated environments.
- **Cons:** Accuracy depends heavily on the quality and representativeness of the source workload profiling. Target storage benchmarks need to be reliable and relevant. Complex I/O patterns can be difficult to model accurately.

27. Database Schema Change Impact Analysis Prediction

- **Explanation:** Making changes to a database schema (e.g., adding/dropping columns, changing data types, modifying relationships) can have unforeseen and disastrous consequences on application performance or functionality if dependent queries or application code are not compatible. AI analyzes the proposed schema change and proactively assesses its potential impact by examining database query logs (to see which queries access the affected tables/columns) and potentially scanning application source code or dependency maps to identify code relying on the current schema structure. It flags high-risk changes that are likely to cause performance degradation or break application functionality.
- **Implementation Strategy:** Requires access to database schema definitions, historical or representative query workload logs, and ideally application source code repositories or pre-computed dependency information. Use AI tools (graph analysis to trace dependencies, simulation to estimate query plan changes, static code analysis parsing) to evaluate the impact of a proposed schema change before it is deployed. Integrate results into change management workflows, highlighting risks to developers and DBAs.
- **Pain Points Addressed:** Deploying schema changes that unexpectedly break applications or cause severe performance regressions, leading to emergency rollbacks and outages.

Time-consuming manual code reviews and testing needed to assess impact. Fear of making necessary schema changes due to potential risks.

- **Key AI Capability: Dependency Graph Analysis, Impact Simulation, Static Code Analysis, Risk Scoring.**
- **Savings/Pros:** Significantly reduces the risk of change-induced database/application failures. Speeds up the deployment process for low-risk schema changes by reducing manual review/testing burden. Encourages safer evolution of database schemas. Improves collaboration between Development and DBA teams by providing objective risk assessment.
- **Cons:** Accurately mapping dependencies, especially through application code, can be very complex and may require specialized code analysis tools. Access to source code might not always be feasible. Effectiveness depends on having representative query workloads. Predictions are not guarantees.

28.Predictive Maintenance for Storage Hardware (Disk, Controller)

- **Explanation:** This is a specific application of predictive hardware failure (1.1 / 1.14) focused DEDICATEDLY on the components within enterprise storage arrays, which often have unique failure modes and telemetry. AI analyzes vendor-specific sensor data and error logs from disks (HDDs and SSDs - e.g., media errors, reallocated sectors, wear leveling counters), controllers (CPU load, memory errors, cache battery health), and other array components to predict failures with higher accuracy than generic server monitoring.
- **Implementation Strategy:** Requires integration with the storage vendor's management platform or APIs to collect detailed, proprietary hardware telemetry and internal error logs. Train AI forecasting or anomaly detection models specifically on the failure precursors for different storage component types (using historical data if available, or vendor-provided models). Integrate alerts into monitoring systems to trigger proactive component replacement, often coordinating with vendor support processes.
- **Pain Points Addressed:** Unexpected failures of critical storage array components (disks, controllers, cache) can lead to performance degradation, data unavailability, or even data loss in severe cases (e.g., multiple concurrent disk failures). Reactive replacement is disruptive.
- **Key AI Capability: Time-Series Forecasting, Anomaly Detection** (applied to specific storage telemetry), **Vendor-Specific Model Integration**.
- **Savings/Pros:** Significantly reduces the risk of data loss or extended downtime due to storage hardware failures (Est: 25-40% fewer failures impact service). Enables proactive, scheduled replacement of failing components, often under warranty/support contracts. Improves overall storage platform stability and reliability.
- **Cons:** Highly dependent on the storage vendor providing access to sufficiently detailed telemetry and error logs. Models may need to be specific to vendor, array model, or even firmware version. Accessing historical failure data for specific components can be difficult.

29. Data Reduction Effectiveness Prediction (Dedupe/Compression)

- **Explanation:** Storage arrays and backup systems offer data reduction techniques like deduplication and compression to save space, but their effectiveness varies greatly depending on the type of data. Before migrating data to a system with these features or enabling them, AI analyzes samples of the actual dataset (or its metadata) to predict the likely data reduction ratio (e.g., 2:1, 5:1) that will be achieved. This helps in making informed decisions about technology adoption and accurate capacity planning.
- **Implementation Strategy:** Involves tools that can scan data samples or analyze file system metadata (file types, sizes). Use AI estimation models or algorithms that understand how different data types (e.g., databases, VMs, text files, encrypted data, already-compressed media files) respond to deduplication and various compression algorithms. Provide an estimated reduction ratio based on the analyzed data mix.
- **Pain Points Addressed:** Uncertainty about the actual storage savings achievable with expensive data reduction technologies, leading to inaccurate ROI calculations or capacity planning. Choosing a storage system based on overly optimistic vendor claims about reduction ratios.
- **Key AI Capability: Classification** (identifying data types), **Estimation Models, Statistical Analysis** (analyzing data entropy and block similarity).
- **Savings/Pros:** Provides more realistic expectations and accurate ROI calculations for investments in data reduction technologies. Helps in selecting the most appropriate storage solution based on actual data characteristics. Leads to more accurate capacity planning and forecasting. Avoids overspending on capacity based on poor reduction estimates.
- **Cons:** Predictions are estimates based on samples or metadata; actual real-world ratios achieved after implementation might vary. Effectiveness depends on the quality of the data sampling or analysis. Different vendor implementations of dedupe/compression can yield different results not fully captured by generic prediction.

30. Automated Database Parameter Tuning Recommendations

- **Explanation:** Databases have hundreds of configuration parameters (controlling memory allocation, parallelism, I/O behavior, optimizer settings etc.). Default settings are often suboptimal, and manual tuning requires deep expertise and iterative experimentation. AI analyzes the specific database workload characteristics, performance metrics, and underlying server resources, then recommends changes to key parameters aimed at improving performance, stability, or resource utilization, often leveraging machine learning trained on previous tuning results or simulation models.
- **Implementation Strategy:** Requires collecting detailed database workload information (query types, frequencies), performance metrics (waits, throughput, cache hits), and server resource specs. Use AI platforms or specialized tools employing optimization algorithms, simulation, or machine learning (e.g., Bayesian optimization, reinforcement learning) to explore the parameter space and suggest optimal settings. Present

recommendations with predicted impact factors for DBA review. Some advanced systems might support automated application of tuning changes in certain contexts.

- **Pain Points Addressed:** Default database parameters often lead to poor performance. Manual tuning is extremely complex, time-consuming, and requires scarce expert skills. Finding the optimal configuration is challenging due to interactions between parameters.
- **Key AI Capability: Optimization** (searching parameter space), **Simulation** (predicting impact of changes), **Machine Learning** (learning optimal settings from experience).
- **Savings/Pros:** Potential for significant database performance and efficiency gains (Est: 10-20%) without code changes. Reduced manual effort and time spent by DBAs on complex tuning tasks. Leads to more consistent and optimized database configurations across the environment.
- **Cons:** Recommendations MUST be validated by expert DBAs before application, as inappropriate parameter changes can severely destabilize a database or cause unexpected negative side effects. AI models may not fully capture all workload nuances or parameter interactions. Effectiveness varies depending on the database platform and the specific workload.

Chapter 5. Category 4: Network Performance & Security (Use Cases)

31. Predictive Network Congestion Detection & Root Cause

- **Explanation:** Network congestion (links or devices becoming overloaded) causes slowdowns, packet loss, and poor application performance. AI analyzes real-time and historical network telemetry - such as bandwidth utilization on router/switch ports (SNMP), network flow data (Netflow/sFlow/IPFIX showing source/destination/protocol), and latency/jitter measurements - to predict when congestion is likely to occur on specific paths *before* it severely impacts traffic. When congestion is detected or predicted, AI also correlates traffic patterns to identify the likely applications, users, or conversations responsible for the overload.
- **Implementation Strategy:** Requires comprehensive network metric collection (SNMP, streaming telemetry) and flow data collection across key network segments. Feed this data into a Network Performance Monitoring (NPM) or AIOps platform with AI capabilities. Use time-series forecasting to predict utilization spikes and anomaly detection to spot unusual traffic patterns. Employ correlation techniques to link congestion events to specific traffic flows identified in Netflow data. Generate alerts identifying the congested path and the likely contributing traffic.
- **Pain Points Addressed:** Network slowdowns impacting critical applications, often reported vaguely by users. Difficulty identifying the specific cause (which application/user/traffic type) of intermittent or building congestion. Reactive response only after performance is already degraded.
- **Key AI Capability: Time-Series Forecasting** (predicting utilization/latency), **Anomaly Detection** (spotting unusual traffic bursts or patterns), **Correlation** (linking congestion metrics to flow data).
- **Savings/Pros:** Enables proactive measures like traffic shaping (QoS), rerouting traffic, or initiating capacity upgrades *before* users are impacted (Est: 30-50% earlier detection). Significantly faster identification of the sources of congestion for mitigation. Reduces application downtime or performance degradation caused by network bottlenecks. Improves overall network reliability.
- **Cons:** Requires investment in widespread network telemetry and flow data collection, which can add overhead. Encrypted traffic can limit visibility into application-specific flows (though flow metadata is still useful). Root cause analysis can still be complex in highly dynamic or multi-layered networks.

32. AI-Driven SD-WAN Path Selection & Optimization

- **Explanation:** Software-Defined Wide Area Networks (SD-WAN) often use multiple underlying transport links (MPLS, broadband internet, LTE). AI enhances SD-WAN controllers by making more intelligent, real-time decisions about which path(s) to use for specific application traffic. It continuously monitors the quality (latency, jitter, packet loss, available bandwidth) of each path and understands the requirements of different applications (e.g., VoIP needs low latency/jitter, bulk backups need high bandwidth). AI selects the optimal path(s) dynamically to maximize performance, ensure reliability (failover), and potentially minimize cost, adapting faster and more intelligently than simple static policies.
- **Implementation Strategy:** Requires an SD-WAN solution where the controller exposes APIs for monitoring path quality and influencing routing decisions, or has built-in AI capabilities. Feed real-time path quality metrics and defined application profiles (performance requirements) into an AI engine. Use reinforcement learning (where the AI learns the best path choices through trial and feedback) or optimization algorithms to make dynamic path selection decisions per application flow or policy group.
- **Pain Points Addressed:** Static SD-WAN policies failing to adapt quickly to changing link conditions. Suboptimal performance for critical applications due to poor path selection. Inefficient use of available WAN links. Difficulty manually tuning complex SD-WAN routing policies.
- **Key AI Capability: Reinforcement Learning** (learning optimal path selection over time), **Optimization** (real-time path selection based on constraints), **Real-time Analytics** (processing link quality data).
- **Savings/Pros:** Measurably improved performance (latency, jitter, loss) for critical applications over the WAN (Est: 10-20% improvement). Better utilization of all available WAN bandwidth, potentially reducing reliance on expensive MPLS. Increased application resilience through faster and smarter failover. Automated optimization reduces manual policy tuning effort.
- **Cons:** High implementation complexity, typically requiring tight integration with or specific features from the SD-WAN vendor. Requires accurate application identification and profiling. AI decision-making might be harder to predict or troubleshoot than static policies initially.

33. Network Device Failure Prediction (Router, Switch, FW)

- **Explanation:** Similar to hardware prediction for servers and storage (1.1, 1.14, 3.8), this focuses specifically on predicting failures in network equipment like routers, switches, firewalls, and load balancers. AI analyzes device-specific telemetry such as syslog messages (looking for specific error patterns), SNMP traps (critical events), environmental sensor readings (temperature, fan speed), CPU/memory utilization trends, and hardware error counters (e.g., interface errors, memory parity errors) to predict impending failures of components like line cards, power supplies, fans, or entire chassis.

- **Implementation Strategy:** Centralize collection of syslog data, SNMP traps, and performance metrics from network devices. Use AI platforms with capabilities for analyzing semi-structured log data (NLP) and time-series metrics. Train forecasting or anomaly detection models based on historical failure data correlated with preceding log messages or metric deviations (often vendor-specific patterns). Generate alerts for proactive investigation or component replacement.
- **Pain Points Addressed:** Network outages are often highly disruptive and costly. Unexpected failures of core network devices can impact large parts of the organization. Reactive replacement is stressful and time-consuming.
- **Key AI Capability: Time-Series Forecasting**, **NLP** (for parsing syslog messages and identifying error patterns), **Anomaly Detection**.
- **Savings/Pros:** Reduces disruptive network outages caused by hardware failures (Est: 20-30% fewer outages). Enables planned, proactive maintenance and replacement of network components. Improves overall network stability and reliability. Reduces emergency shipping and labor costs.
- **Cons:** Failure precursors and log messages indicating problems vary significantly between network vendors and device models, requiring potentially many specific models. Accessing sufficient historical failure data for training can be challenging. Requires comprehensive logging and monitoring setup for network devices.

34. Network Security Anomaly Detection (Lateral Movement, C&C)

- **Explanation:** This AI application focuses on detecting malicious activities *within* the network that might bypass perimeter defenses. By analyzing network traffic patterns (primarily from flow data like Netflow/IPFIX, but also DNS logs, firewall logs, proxy logs), AI establishes baselines of normal communication (who talks to whom, using which protocols, at what volume, at what times). It then detects significant deviations indicative of attacks, such as: a compromised host scanning the internal network (lateral movement), communication with known malicious command-and-control (C&C) servers, unusual data transfers suggesting exfiltration, or anomalous DNS query patterns.
- **Implementation Strategy:** Requires broad collection of network flow data, DNS logs, and potentially firewall/proxy logs, feeding into a Security Information and Event Management (SIEM), Network Detection and Response (NDR), or security analytics platform. Use AI techniques like anomaly detection (statistical outliers, behavioral deviations), graph analysis (visualizing communication patterns and spotting unusual links), and machine learning classification (trained on known malicious patterns) correlated with threat intelligence feeds. Generate high-fidelity security alerts for the Security Operations Center (SOC).
- **Pain Points Addressed:** Sophisticated attackers often operate stealthily inside the network for extended periods ("dwell time"). Traditional signature-based detection

misses novel or polymorphic threats. Difficulty distinguishing malicious traffic from legitimate traffic in high-volume networks.

- **Key AI Capability: Anomaly Detection** (behavioral baselining), **Graph Analysis** (mapping communication flows), **Machine Learning Classification, Threat Intelligence Correlation**.
- **Savings/Pros:** Enables earlier detection of active breaches and compromised systems. Significantly reduces attacker dwell time and potential damage/data loss. Helps uncover threats missed by traditional security tools. Provides valuable context for incident response.
- **Cons:** Can generate false positives, requiring tuning and investigation by skilled security analysts. Encrypted internal traffic limits visibility for some techniques (though metadata analysis is still useful). Requires significant data storage and processing power. Effectiveness depends on the quality of baselining and threat intelligence.

35. Firewall Rule Optimization & Cleanup Recommendations

- **Explanation:** Firewall rulesets tend to grow over time, becoming complex, inefficient, and potentially insecure. AI analyzes firewall configuration policies along with traffic logs (or rule hit counters) to identify various types of problematic rules: **redundant** rules (identical effect to another rule), **shadowed** rules (placed after a broader rule that always catches the traffic first, so they are never hit), **overly permissive** rules (allowing more access than necessary), **unused** rules (zero hit counts over an extended period), or conflicting rules. It provides specific recommendations for removal, modification, or reordering to simplify the ruleset, improve performance, and reduce the attack surface.
- **Implementation Strategy:** Ingest firewall configuration files/APIs and traffic logs or hit count data into a specialized firewall management or security analytics tool. Use AI algorithms based on rule logic analysis, pattern matching, and correlation with traffic data to identify the problematic rules. Present clear recommendations for cleanup actions to firewall administrators, often with explanations and potential impact assessment.
- **Pain Points Addressed:** Complex and bloated firewall rulesets are hard to manage, audit, and troubleshoot. Unnecessary rules can degrade firewall performance. Overly permissive or shadowed rules create security risks. Difficulty identifying and safely removing obsolete rules.
- **Key AI Capability: Rule Logic Analysis, Optimization, Pattern Recognition, Data Correlation** (rules vs. traffic).
- **Savings/Pros:** Reduces the network attack surface by eliminating unnecessary openings. Improves firewall performance by shrinking the ruleset size. Simplifies firewall management, auditing, and troubleshooting. Increases confidence in the security posture enforced by the firewall. Helps enforce "least privilege" principles.
- **Cons:** Recommendations require careful validation by experienced firewall administrators before implementation, as removing a rule incorrectly could break legitimate application connectivity. Understanding the original *intent* behind a rule can

sometimes be challenging solely from logs and config. Requires access to both configuration and traffic/hit data.

36. Automated Micro-segmentation Policy Generation/Validation

- **Explanation:** Micro-segmentation (implementing fine-grained network security controls, often down to the individual workload level, based on Zero Trust principles) is powerful but extremely complex to implement manually. AI helps by analyzing actual network communication flows between applications and workloads. Based on these observed flows, it automatically generates a baseline set of "allow" policies (e.g., firewall rules) required for the application to function correctly. This provides a starting point for micro-segmentation policy, drastically reducing manual effort. AI can also continuously validate existing policies against actual traffic, flagging violations or unused rules.
- **Implementation Strategy:** Requires deploying tools that provide visibility into workload-to-workload communication flows (e.g., agents on hosts, instrumentation in service mesh, flow data from hypervisors/network). Feed this flow data into a micro-segmentation platform or security policy tool with AI capabilities. Use AI (graph analysis, clustering, classification) to map dependencies and generate least-privilege policy recommendations. Integrate generated policies with enforcement points (host firewalls, security groups, infrastructure firewalls). Implement ongoing validation mode.
- **Pain Points Addressed:** Defining and maintaining granular micro-segmentation policies manually is prohibitively complex, slow, and error-prone, hindering Zero Trust adoption. Fear of breaking applications by implementing overly restrictive policies. Difficulty visualizing application communication patterns.
- **Key AI Capability: Graph Analysis** (mapping flows), **Classification** (grouping workloads), **Policy Generation/Recommendation, Traffic Flow Analysis**.
- **Savings/Pros:** Dramatically accelerates the adoption of micro-segmentation and Zero Trust architectures (Est: 50%+ faster policy definition). Reduces the risk of human error in complex policy creation. Provides a data-driven baseline for least-privilege access. Enhances security by limiting lateral movement for attackers. Improves application dependency understanding.
- **Cons:** Requires excellent visibility into inter-workload traffic flows. Generated policies are often a starting point and usually require refinement and exception handling by security teams. Discovering all necessary flows, especially for infrequent communication paths (like DR), can be challenging.

37. Network Capacity Planning Based on Predicted Demand

- **Explanation:** Similar to general capacity planning (1.10), but specifically focused on network links (e.g., internet circuits, WAN links connecting sites, data center interconnects, cloud direct connections). AI analyzes historical bandwidth utilization trends on these key links, considers business growth projections, planned application deployments, or expected traffic shifts (e.g., cloud migrations), and uses forecasting models to predict future bandwidth requirements, enabling proactive upgrades or new circuit provisioning.

- **Implementation Strategy:** Collect and store long-term (months/years) bandwidth utilization metrics (e.g., 95th percentile, average/peak bps) for critical network links. Integrate business forecast data or project pipeline information where available. Apply time-series forecasting models tuned for network traffic patterns. Generate regular capacity planning reports showing predicted utilization vs. capacity and estimated exhaustion dates.
- **Pain Points Addressed:** Network links becoming saturated unexpectedly, causing widespread performance issues. Overspending on excessive network bandwidth that goes unused. Lack of data-driven justification for expensive network upgrades. Reactive and lengthy circuit provisioning cycles.
- **Key AI Capability: Time-Series Forecasting, Trend Analysis.**
- **Savings/Pros:** Ensures network capacity keeps pace with business demand, preventing performance bottlenecks. Optimizes spending on network circuits by avoiding unnecessary over-provisioning (Est: 10-20% improved utilization). Provides data-driven justification for budget requests for network upgrades. Allows sufficient lead time for potentially long circuit provisioning processes.
- **Cons:** Accuracy depends on the predictability of traffic growth (major unexpected events are hard to forecast). Requires consistent long-term data collection. Integrating qualitative business projections (e.g., "new app launch") into quantitative forecasts needs careful modeling.

38. WAN Latency Fluctuation Prediction & Explanation

- **Explanation:** Intermittent spikes in Wide Area Network (WAN) latency or jitter can severely impact real-time applications (VoIP, video conferencing, VDI) but are often hard to diagnose. AI analyzes patterns in continuous latency/jitter measurements taken across WAN paths (using active probes). It attempts to predict recurring spikes (e.g., correlating with specific times of day or days of week) and potentially explain them by correlating latency fluctuations with other events like BGP routing changes (if BGP data is available), known ISP maintenance windows or outages (if feeds are available), or even large internal data transfers that might saturate links.
- **Implementation Strategy:** Deploy active network monitoring agents (probes) at key sites performing frequent end-to-end latency, jitter, and loss measurements across WAN paths. Feed this detailed measurement data into an NPM or AIOps platform. Use AI (anomaly detection, time-series analysis, correlation engines) to identify patterns and correlate latency events with other data sources (BGP feeds, ISP reports, internal traffic data). Provide insights or alerts about predictable fluctuations or likely causes.
- **Pain Points Addressed:** Frustrating, hard-to-diagnose intermittent performance issues for applications sensitive to latency/jitter over the WAN. Difficulty holding ISPs accountable without clear data patterns. Wasted troubleshooting time on transient issues.

- **Key AI Capability: Anomaly Detection, Correlation, Time-Series Analysis, Pattern Recognition**.
- **Savings/Pros:** Faster identification of patterns causing intermittent WAN issues. Provides better data for discussing chronic problems with ISP providers. Helps distinguish between internal network issues and external provider problems. Potentially allows scheduling less sensitive traffic around predictable high-latency periods.
- **Cons:** Root cause of WAN latency often lies within ISP networks, offering limited visibility and control. Access to reliable ISP outage/maintenance data or BGP feeds can be difficult or expensive. Correlation doesn't always prove causation.

39. Automated Network Troubleshooting Path Analysis

- **Explanation:** When a user reports "I can't reach server X," network engineers typically perform a manual sequence of steps: traceroute, ping, checking DNS, checking firewall rules on intermediate devices, verifying routing tables, checking device status, etc. AI automates this diagnostic workflow. Based on the source and destination, it orchestrates the execution of these diagnostic commands across the relevant network devices along the likely path, analyzes the results, and pinpoints the probable location and nature of the connectivity failure (e.g., "Firewall rule blocking traffic at FW-Core-01," "Routing loop detected near Router-Edge-03," "Destination server unresponsive").
- **Implementation Strategy:** Requires a platform (often integrated within NPM or network automation tools) with secure credential access to network devices (via SSH, SNMP, APIs). Define diagnostic workflows based on standard troubleshooting procedures. Use AI path analysis algorithms (leveraging topology data from 1.7 or device routing tables) to determine the relevant devices to query. Orchestrate command execution and use NLP or pattern matching to interpret the results, synthesizing them into a clear diagnosis.
- **Pain Points Addressed:** Manual network connectivity troubleshooting is repetitive, time-consuming, and requires skilled engineers. Delays in diagnosing simple connectivity issues impact users and application availability. Inconsistent troubleshooting steps lead to missed issues.
- **Key AI Capability: Workflow Automation, Path Analysis Algorithms, Network Topology Awareness, NLP/Pattern Matching** (interpreting command outputs).
- **Savings/Pros:** Dramatically reduces the time taken to diagnose common network connectivity problems (Est: 60-80% faster). Frees up experienced network engineers from routine troubleshooting tasks. Ensures consistent and thorough diagnostic steps are followed every time. Can be integrated with service desk tools for initial automated diagnosis.
- **Cons:** Requires providing the automation platform with broad access credentials to network devices, which needs careful security consideration. Complex network designs (NAT, overlays, complex firewall policies) can make path determination and result interpretation challenging. Initial setup of workflows and device integrations can be significant.

40.VPN Performance Degradation Prediction & Root Cause

- **Explanation:** Poor performance over Virtual Private Networks (VPNs) is a common complaint from remote workers. AI analyzes performance metrics from VPN concentrators (CPU/memory load, tunnel counts, throughput), user endpoints (if available via agent - e.g., client-side latency, local network conditions), and potentially general internet weather data or ISP performance reports. It aims to predict periods of likely VPN degradation (e.g., during peak login times) and diagnose the root cause when issues occur - distinguishing between overloaded VPN hardware, widespread ISP problems affecting many users in a region, or issues specific to an individual user's connection.

- **Implementation Strategy:** Collect metrics/logs from VPN concentrators. Optionally deploy endpoint agents on remote user devices to gather client-side performance data. Integrate ISP performance data or internet weather reports if possible. Feed this diverse data into an AIOps or NPM platform. Use AI (forecasting, correlation, clustering) to predict load-based issues on concentrators, identify clusters of users experiencing similar problems (suggesting regional ISP issues), and flag potential individual user connection problems.

- **Pain Points Addressed:** Frequent complaints about slow or unreliable VPN performance impacting remote productivity. Difficulty diagnosing whether VPN issues are systemic (IT's problem) or localized (user's home network/ISP problem). Inefficient use of support resources troubleshooting individual user connections when the issue is broader.

- **Key AI Capability: Forecasting** (predicting concentrator load), **Correlation** (linking user complaints to metrics), **Clustering** (grouping users with similar issues/locations).

- **Savings/Pros:** Enables proactive scaling or optimization of VPN infrastructure based on predicted demand. Faster diagnosis of the scope and likely cause of VPN performance issues (systemic vs. local). Improved communication with users regarding widespread issues. More efficient allocation of support resources. Overall improved remote work experience.

- **Cons:** Limited visibility and control over users' home networks and local ISP performance remain major challenges. Collecting data from user endpoints requires agent deployment and raises privacy considerations. Reliable ISP performance data is often difficult to obtain.

Chapter 6. Category 5: Cloud Operations & FinOps (Use Cases)

41.Predictive Cloud Spend Forecasting (Service, Tag, Account)

- **Explanation:** Cloud bills can fluctuate significantly and unexpectedly. AI analyzes detailed historical cloud billing and usage data, recognizing patterns, trends (growth rates), and seasonality (e.g., higher usage at month-end). It uses this to generate statistically robust forecasts of future spending, typically projecting daily, weekly, or monthly costs broken down by specific cloud services (EC2, S3, RDS), application or cost center (using resource tags), and potentially by individual accounts or projects.
- **Implementation Strategy:** Requires automated ingestion of fine-grained cloud billing reports (e.g., AWS Cost and Usage Report - CUR, Azure Cost Management exports) into a FinOps platform, data lake, or BI tool. Apply sophisticated time-series forecasting models (like ARIMA, Prophet, or deep learning models like LSTM) that can handle multiple seasonalities and trends. Ensure data cleansing and proper handling of tags for accurate breakdown. Present forecasts via dashboards and reports accessible to Finance, FinOps, and budget owners.
- **Pain Points Addressed:** Unexpectedly high cloud bills causing budget variances ("bill shock"). Difficulty in accurately planning and budgeting for cloud consumption. Lack of visibility into future cost trends for specific projects or services. Manual forecasting based on simple extrapolations is often inaccurate.
- **Key AI Capability: Time-Series Forecasting, Trend Analysis, Seasonality Detection.**
- **Savings/Pros:** Enables much more accurate cloud budget planning and financial control (Est: 90-95% monthly forecast accuracy). Provides early warning if spending trends deviate significantly from forecasts (linking to 5.6). Allows for proactive cost optimization discussions based on projected spend. Improves financial predictability for cloud operations.
- **Cons:** Accuracy relies heavily on clean, consistent, and sufficiently long historical billing data. Requires consistent and accurate resource tagging for meaningful breakdowns. Cannot easily predict costs associated with entirely new service deployments or major, unannounced architectural changes without manual input. Models need periodic retraining.

42.RI/Savings Plan Purchase & Modification Recommendations

- **Explanation:** Cloud providers offer significant discounts via commitment instruments like Reserved Instances (RIs) and Savings Plans (SPs) where you commit to a certain level of usage for 1 or 3 years. Determining the *optimal* commitment level and type (e.g.,

Standard vs. Convertible RI, Compute vs. EC2 Instance SP) is complex. AI analyzes granular usage data (typically hourly instance usage) over a relevant period, simulates different commitment purchase scenarios against current pricing models, and recommends the specific portfolio of RIs/SPs that maximizes savings while minimizing the risk of paying for unused committed resources. It can also recommend modifications (e.g., converting RIs) or trades on the RI marketplace.

- **Implementation Strategy:** Requires ingesting detailed, hourly compute usage data (instance type, region, OS, tenancy) and current RI/SP pricing information via cloud provider APIs. Use sophisticated optimization algorithms (often involving linear programming or specialized heuristics) and simulation engines within a FinOps platform or dedicated tool. The AI models potential future usage variability and calculates break-even points. Present clear, actionable recommendations (e.g., "Buy 10 m5.xlarge 1-yr All Upfront Standard RIs in us-east-1," "Increase Compute Savings Plan commitment by $5/hr").
- **Pain Points Addressed:** Missing substantial savings opportunities by under-committing. Wasting money by over-committing and leaving purchased RIs/SPs unused. Complexity of choosing between numerous RI/SP types, terms, and payment options across different instance families and regions. Manual analysis is extremely time-consuming and error-prone.
- **Key AI Capability: Optimization** (finding best commitment portfolio), **Simulation** (modeling cost under different scenarios), **Usage Pattern Analysis**.
- **Savings/Pros:** Maximizes achievable discounts from cloud provider commitments (Est: Often achieve 80-95% of theoretical maximum savings vs. much lower with manual efforts). Reduces financial risk associated with commitment purchases. Provides data-driven justification for large commitment expenditures. Frees up FinOps analysts from complex manual calculations.
- **Cons:** Requires very granular (hourly) usage data over a significant period (weeks/months). Cloud provider pricing and commitment offerings change frequently, requiring continuous updates to the AI models/tools. Recommendations still require human review and business judgment regarding future plans.

43.Cross-Cloud/Region Workload Placement Optimization (Cost/Perf)

- **Explanation:** For organizations utilizing multiple public clouds (multi-cloud) or multiple regions within a single cloud, AI helps determine the most advantageous location to run specific workloads. It analyzes the workload's requirements (CPU/RAM needs, performance sensitivity, data residency/compliance constraints, latency needs relative to users or other services) and compares these against the constantly changing costs (compute, storage, data egress fees), performance benchmarks, and available services across different cloud providers and regions. It recommends the optimal placement to minimize cost while meeting performance and compliance needs.
- **Implementation Strategy:** Requires defining detailed profiles for workloads, including performance, compliance, and data interaction constraints. Ingest real-time or

frequently updated pricing information, performance benchmark data, inter-region/inter-cloud latency data, and data egress cost structures from relevant cloud providers/regions. Use multi-objective optimization algorithms to find the best placement that balances cost, performance, and constraint satisfaction. Recommendations can feed into migration planning or automated provisioning/orchestration systems.

- **Pain Points Addressed:** Running workloads in unnecessarily expensive cloud regions or providers. Suboptimal application performance due to high latency to users or dependent services. Difficulty ensuring compliance with data residency regulations in a distributed environment. Complex manual decision-making for workload placement.
- **Key AI Capability: Optimization** (multi-objective: cost, performance, compliance), **Simulation, Constraint Programming, Data Aggregation** (cross-cloud pricing/performance).
- **Savings/Pros:** Potential for significant operating cost reduction in multi-cloud/multi-region environments (Est: 10-25% on optimized workloads). Improved application performance and user experience through latency-aware placement. Automated enforcement of data residency and compliance constraints. Data-driven architectural decisions.
- **Cons:** High implementation complexity, requiring sophisticated modeling and continuous ingestion of diverse, dynamic data from multiple sources. Data egress costs can be a major factor and complex to model accurately. Frequent automated re-balancing of workloads across regions/clouds can introduce operational complexity and potential disruption if not managed carefully.

44. Automated Unused/Orphaned Resource Identification & Termination

- **Explanation:** Cloud environments often accumulate unused resources over time - VMs stopped but never terminated, unattached persistent disks/volumes, unassigned elastic IPs, idle load balancers, old snapshots, etc. These "zombie" resources incur ongoing costs and can represent potential security risks. AI scans the cloud inventory and utilization metrics, using predefined rules and anomaly detection to identify resources that show zero or near-zero activity over an extended period, lack ownership tags, or appear detached from any active application or service. It flags these resources for review and potential automated termination/cleanup.
- **Implementation Strategy:** Integrate a FinOps or cloud governance tool with cloud provider APIs to continuously pull resource inventory and utilization metrics (CPU, network I/O, disk I/O, attachment status). Define rules and train AI models (e.g., anomaly detection looking for prolonged inactivity, pattern recognition for detached resources) to identify potential waste based on configurable thresholds (e.g., "VM idle for >30 days," "Disk unattached for >14 days"). Generate reports or alerts for owners/admins, or trigger automated tagging ("Marked for Deletion") or termination workflows after an approval or grace period.

- **Pain Points Addressed:** "Cloud sprawl" and resource clutter making environments hard to manage. Significant wasted spend on forgotten or idle resources ("cost leakage"). Potential security exposures from unmanaged, unpatched resources. Manual cleanup efforts are tedious and often incomplete.
- **Key AI Capability: Pattern Recognition, Anomaly Detection** (zero/low utilization), **Rule Engines, Workflow Automation** (for cleanup).
- **Savings/Pros:** Direct and often immediate cost savings by eliminating payment for unused resources (Est: 5-15% of cloud spend is common waste). Reduces the potential attack surface by removing unmanaged assets. Leads to a cleaner, more manageable cloud environment. Frees up IP addresses and other limited quotas.
- **Cons:** High risk of accidentally terminating needed resources if rules or AI models are too aggressive or lack context (e.g., a DR resource intentionally kept idle). Requires careful validation procedures, clear ownership definition (tagging), and often human review before termination, especially initially. Determining true "orphaned" status can sometimes be ambiguous.

45. Intelligent Resource Tagging & Compliance Validation

- **Explanation:** Consistent and accurate resource tagging (e.g., applying labels like 'CostCenter:Finance', 'Application:Payroll', 'Owner:jdoe', 'Environment:Prod') is crucial for cost allocation, automation, and governance in the cloud. AI assists by suggesting appropriate tags based on resource names, network placement, associated resources, or even analyzing workload characteristics. It can also use NLP to parse tags entered manually and check for conformity with predefined naming conventions or required tag formats. Furthermore, AI continuously scans resources and validates whether they possess the mandatory tags required by organizational governance policies, flagging non-compliant resources.
- **Implementation Strategy:** Define a clear organizational tagging strategy and policy (which tags are mandatory, naming conventions, allowed values). Use cloud governance tools or custom scripts integrated with AI services (NLP, classification). Train models to suggest tags based on resource attributes or context. Implement policy checks (often using rule engines or simple AI classification) that scan resources via cloud APIs and compare existing tags against the policy requirements. Generate compliance reports or trigger automated remediation (e.g., notifying owner, quarantining resource).
- **Pain Points Addressed:** Inconsistent, missing, or inaccurate tags making cost allocation impossible or unreliable. Difficulty enforcing tagging policies manually across large environments. Automation scripts failing due to missing tags. Inability to group resources logically for reporting or security policies.
- **Key AI Capability: NLP** (parsing names, suggesting tags), **Classification** (validating tag values), **Pattern Recognition** (identifying context for tag suggestion), **Policy Engines** (checking compliance).
- **Savings/Pros:** Enables accurate cost allocation, showback, and chargeback. Improves governance and accountability (Est: achieve 95%+ tagging compliance). Facilitates

reliable automation based on tags (e.g., patching Prod servers). Allows for effective resource grouping for security, backup, or reporting purposes. Reduces manual effort in enforcing tagging standards.

- **Cons:** Requires a well-defined and communicated tagging strategy as a prerequisite. AI suggestions need review. Enforcing mandatory tags on existing untagged resources can be a significant remediation effort. Effectiveness depends on consistent naming conventions and resource context.

46. Cloud Budget Anomaly Detection & Alerting

- **Explanation:** This focuses on catching unexpected deviations in cloud spending *as they happen* or shortly thereafter, rather than waiting for the monthly bill. AI continuously monitors near real-time or daily cloud cost data, compares it against established forecasts (from 5.1) or learned normal spending patterns for that time period, and triggers immediate alerts if significant, statistically relevant anomalies (spikes or drops) are detected. Alerts typically pinpoint the specific service, region, or tagged resource group responsible for the deviation.
- **Implementation Strategy:** Requires setting up frequent (ideally daily or near real-time) ingestion of cloud cost data, often via cloud provider APIs or specific budget/alerting services (e.g., AWS Budgets, Azure Cost Alerts). Feed this data into an anomaly detection engine within a FinOps tool or AIOps platform. Configure alerting thresholds based on statistical significance or percentage deviation from forecast/baseline. Route alerts to relevant budget owners, FinOps team, or engineers via appropriate channels (email, Slack, PagerDuty).
- **Pain Points Addressed:** Discovering massive, unexpected cost overruns (e.g., due to a deployment error, misconfiguration, or attack) only weeks later when the bill arrives, making mitigation harder and costs higher. Lack of timely visibility into spending deviations.
- **Key AI Capability: Anomaly Detection** (applied to cost time-series data), **Forecasting** (providing the baseline for comparison).
- **Savings/Pros:** Enables extremely rapid detection (within hours or a day) of potentially costly issues like runaway resource provisioning, configuration errors, or resource-intensive attacks. Allows for immediate investigation and corrective action, minimizing financial damage. Provides tight control over cloud budgets. Increases cost accountability.
- **Cons:** Can be sensitive to normal fluctuations or legitimate but unplanned usage, requiring careful tuning of alert thresholds to avoid excessive noise. Requires access to near real-time cost data, which might have limitations or delays depending on the cloud provider and tools used.

47. Automated Cloud Service Dependency Mapping for Cost Allocation

- **Explanation:** Accurately allocating the costs of shared cloud services (e.g., a central Kubernetes cluster, shared databases, data transfer costs, monitoring tools) to the specific applications or business units consuming them is a major FinOps challenge. AI helps by analyzing data like network traffic flows between applications and shared services, API call logs, resource tags, and application architecture information (if available) to automatically map these dependencies and estimate the proportional consumption of shared resources by different consumers, enabling more equitable cost allocation.

- **Implementation Strategy:** Requires collecting data sources that reveal interactions: VPC flow logs, cloud provider network monitoring, API Gateway logs, CloudTrail/Audit Logs, and leveraging consistent application/service tagging. Use graph analysis techniques to build dependency maps showing which applications communicate with which shared services. Apply correlation or statistical methods to estimate resource consumption based on traffic volume, API call frequency, or other relevant metrics. Integrate these derived allocation keys into FinOps reporting or chargeback models.

- **Pain Points Addressed:** Difficulty fairly and accurately allocating the costs of shared cloud infrastructure or platform services. Simple allocation methods (e.g., equal split) are often inaccurate and unfair, leading to disputes. Lack of visibility into which applications are driving shared service costs.

- **Key AI Capability: Graph Analysis** (mapping dependencies), **Correlation, Network Flow Analysis, Data Integration**.

- **Savings/Pros:** Enables much more accurate and defensible showback or chargeback for shared services. Provides clear visibility into the true Total Cost of Ownership (TCO) for applications. Encourages application teams to be more mindful of their consumption of shared resources. Informs architectural decisions regarding shared vs. dedicated resources.

- **Cons:** High implementation complexity, requiring collation and analysis of diverse and potentially large datasets (especially network flows). Accuracy depends heavily on the quality and completeness of interaction data and tagging. Allocating costs based purely on usage might not always reflect business value perfectly. Encryption can limit visibility into API calls or traffic content.

48. Showback/Chargeback Report Automation & Optimization

- **Explanation:** Manually creating detailed cost reports for different business units, application teams, or projects, showing their specific cloud consumption and allocated shared costs, is time-consuming and prone to errors. AI/automation streamlines this by ingesting the processed and tagged cost data (potentially enriched with allocation keys from 5.7), applying defined reporting rules and formatting, and automatically generating customized reports on a regular schedule. NLP might be used optionally to add narrative summaries or highlight key cost drivers and optimization recommendations within the reports.

- **Implementation Strategy:** Requires having clean, tagged, and potentially allocated cost data available in a FinOps platform or data warehouse. Define report templates and distribution lists for different stakeholders. Use automation tools (BI platforms with scheduling, dedicated FinOps reporting tools, or custom scripts) to generate and distribute reports. Optionally integrate NLP generation models (trained on financial summaries) to create automated commentary.
- **Pain Points Addressed:** Significant manual effort spent by FinOps or finance teams each month creating and distributing cost reports. Reports are often delayed, inconsistent, or contain errors. Lack of timely cost visibility for budget owners hinders accountability.
- **Key AI Capability: Report Generation Automation, Workflow Automation, Data Aggregation**, optional **NLP (Text Generation)**.
- **Savings/Pros:** Dramatically reduces manual effort and time spent on reporting (Est: 80%+ reduction). Ensures timely, consistent, and accurate cost visibility for stakeholders. Improves cost accountability across the organization. Frees up FinOps team for higher-value analysis and optimization activities. Enhanced stakeholder satisfaction.
- **Cons:** Quality of automated reports depends entirely on the quality and granularity of the input cost data (tagging accuracy, allocation method effectiveness). NLP-generated summaries require careful validation for accuracy and appropriate tone. Custom report requirements might still need specific development.

49. Cost Impact Simulation for Architectural Changes (Cloud)

- **Explanation:** Before committing to building or migrating an application with a specific architecture in the cloud, architects and engineers can use AI-powered simulation tools to estimate the likely operational cost. They define the proposed architecture (e.g., types and number of VMs, database services, load balancers, storage types) and provide estimates of expected usage (e.g., traffic levels, data volumes, transaction rates). The AI tool then uses current cloud pricing models and simulation techniques to project the monthly or annual cost under different scenarios, allowing for comparison of architectural alternatives and identification of potential cost hotspots early in the design phase.
- **Implementation Strategy:** Utilize cloud provider cost calculators, third-party FinOps tools with modeling capabilities, or custom-built simulation engines. Requires integration with cloud provider pricing APIs to ensure up-to-date cost information. Users input architectural components and estimated usage parameters. The AI simulation model calculates costs based on pricing rules (including data transfer, API calls, etc.) and usage estimates. Output includes projected costs, potentially broken down by component, and sensitivity analysis (how costs change if usage estimates vary).
- **Pain Points Addressed:** Making architectural decisions without a clear understanding of their long-term cost implications. Receiving unexpectedly high cloud bills after deploying

a new or migrated application. Difficulty comparing the cost-effectiveness of different cloud services or architectural patterns (e.g., serverless vs. containers vs. VMs).

- **Key AI Capability: Simulation, Cost Modeling, What-if Analysis.**
- **Savings/Pros:** Enables architects to make cost-aware design decisions *before* implementation, potentially avoiding significant long-term expense. Provides more realistic cost estimates for project budgeting and business cases. Helps identify and optimize high-cost components early in the lifecycle. Facilitates comparison of different architectural options on a cost basis.
- **Cons:** Accuracy is highly dependent on the quality and realism of the usage estimates provided by the user ("Garbage In, Garbage Out"). Cloud pricing models are complex and constantly changing, requiring diligent updates to the simulator. Does not easily account for unpredictable usage spikes or future price changes.

50. Cloud Migration Wave Planning Optimization

- **Explanation:** Migrating hundreds or thousands of applications to the cloud requires careful planning of which applications move when (migration "waves"). AI can optimize this complex planning process by considering multiple factors simultaneously: **technical dependencies** between applications (must migrate DB before dependent App), **business criticality** (migrate revenue-generating apps sooner?), **migration team capacity** and skills, **technical complexity** of migrating each app, and potential **cost savings** achievable post-migration. AI suggests optimal groupings and sequencing of applications into migration waves to minimize risk, reduce overall migration duration, ensure dependencies are met, and potentially accelerate realization of benefits.
- **Implementation Strategy:** Requires comprehensive data gathering: application inventory, detailed inter-application dependency mapping (often a major challenge, potentially aided by tools like 1.7 or 4.7), business criticality ratings, estimates of migration effort/complexity per application, and data on migration team availability/skills. Use AI optimization algorithms (like clustering for grouping, scheduling algorithms considering dependencies and resource constraints) within a dedicated migration planning tool or via custom modeling. Output is a recommended wave plan (applications per wave, sequence of waves).
- **Pain Points Addressed:** Migration planning done manually is subjective, prone to errors, and often fails to account for complex dependencies, leading to delays, rework, and unexpected outages during migration. Inefficient sequencing can prolong the migration timeline and delay benefits. Overloading migration teams.
- **Key AI Capability: Optimization** (grouping and sequencing), **Dependency Analysis** (graph-based), **Clustering, Scheduling Algorithms, Constraint Programming**.
- **Savings/Pros:** Creates a more data-driven, efficient, and lower-risk migration plan (Est: 10-20% reduction in timeline vs. ad-hoc planning). Ensures technical dependencies are respected, reducing migration failures. Balances workload across migration teams. Helps prioritize waves based on strategic goals (e.g., cost savings, retiring specific DC). Improves predictability of the migration program.

- **Cons:** Very high complexity due to the need for extensive and accurate input data, especially application dependencies which are often poorly documented. Optimization models can be complex to build and tune. The plan is only as good as the input data and assumptions. Still requires human oversight and adjustment based on qualitative factors.

Chapter 7. Category 6: Security Ops & Threat Intelligence (Use Cases)

51.AI-Powered User & Entity Behavior Analytics (UEBA)

- **Explanation:** UEBA focuses on detecting threats originating from *within* the environment, which often bypass traditional defenses. AI builds dynamic behavioral baselines for individual users (login times/locations, resources accessed, data volumes transferred) and system entities (servers initiating unusual connections, processes exhibiting strange behavior). It then continuously monitors activity, using machine learning to identify statistically significant deviations from these established norms. Such anomalies could indicate a compromised user account being used by an attacker, malicious insider activity, or even malware acting atypically.

- **Implementation Strategy:** Requires ingestion of large volumes of diverse log data into a dedicated UEBA platform or an advanced SIEM with UEBA capabilities. Key data sources include: Authentication logs (Active Directory, VPN, cloud IAM), endpoint logs (process activity, file access), network flow data, cloud provider activity logs (CloudTrail, Azure Activity Log), and potentially HR data (for context like role changes, terminations). AI uses unsupervised machine learning (clustering, anomaly detection) and sometimes supervised learning (trained on known attack patterns) to build profiles and detect deviations. Alerts are typically risk-scored based on the severity and number of anomalies observed for a user/entity, feeding into SOC investigation queues.

- **Pain Points Addressed:** Difficulty detecting compromised credentials (stolen passwords) being used by attackers, as they appear "legitimate." Identifying malicious insiders who misuse their authorized access. Detecting low-and-slow attacks that don't trigger obvious signatures. Alert fatigue from overly sensitive rules.

- **Key AI Capability: Anomaly Detection** (primary), **Behavioral Profiling/Modeling, Machine Learning (Clustering, Classification), Risk Scoring**.

- **Savings/Pros:** Enables early detection of threats that bypass perimeter and signature-based defenses, significantly reducing attacker dwell time and potential breach impact. Particularly effective against insider threats and credential theft. Provides context-rich alerts focused on high-risk entities rather than isolated events. Helps prioritize investigations for the SOC.

- **Cons:** Can be data-intensive and computationally expensive. Prone to generating false positives, especially during the initial learning phase or when user roles/behaviors change legitimately, requiring significant tuning by analysts. Privacy concerns need careful management due to monitoring user activity. Effectiveness depends on the breadth and quality of ingested log data.

52. Automated Phishing Email Detection & Triage

- **Explanation:** Phishing remains a primary attack vector. AI significantly enhances email security gateways or analysis tools by going beyond simple keyword matching or sender reputation checks. It uses Natural Language Processing (NLP) to analyze email content for subtle signs of social engineering (urgency, unusual requests), examines URL destinations for malicious indicators (domain age, reputation, visual similarity to legitimate sites via image recognition on landing pages), scrutinizes attachments using static and dynamic analysis (similar to 6.8), and correlates findings with threat intelligence feeds. The goal is to automatically identify and block/quarantine malicious emails with high accuracy, reducing user exposure and the manual triage burden on security teams.

- **Implementation Strategy:** Typically involves deploying an AI-enhanced Secure Email Gateway (SEG) solution, adding AI capabilities to an existing SEG, or integrating a specialized AI phishing analysis tool with the email system (often via API for analyzing reported emails). Requires training robust AI models (NLP classifiers, computer vision models) on massive datasets of phishing and legitimate emails. Must integrate seamlessly with email flow for automated blocking/quarantining and potentially with SOAR tools (6.6) for automated incident response actions based on confirmed phishing attempts.

- **Pain Points Addressed:** High volume of phishing emails reaching user inboxes. Users falling victim to increasingly sophisticated phishing attacks. Security teams overwhelmed manually analyzing user-reported suspicious emails. Signature-based defenses easily bypassed by attackers.

- **Key AI Capability: Natural Language Processing (NLP)** (analyzing text for intent/deception), **Classification** (phishing vs. legitimate), **Image Recognition/Computer Vision** (analyzing website screenshots), **Threat Intelligence Correlation, Malware Analysis** (for attachments).

- **Savings/Pros:** Significantly higher detection rate for sophisticated phishing attempts compared to traditional methods (Est: 95%+ accuracy claimed by leading vendors). Drastically reduces the number of malicious emails reaching users. Frees up significant SOC analyst time previously spent on manual email triage. Faster response to emerging phishing campaigns. Reduced risk of credential theft and malware infection via email.

- **Cons:** No solution is 100% foolproof; highly targeted or novel attacks can still slip through. False positives (blocking legitimate emails) can occur and impact business communication, requiring careful tuning and allow-listing processes. Requires continuous model updates to keep pace with evolving attacker techniques. Dependent on vendor capabilities and threat intelligence quality.

53. AI-Driven Vulnerability Prioritization (Beyond CVSS)

- **Explanation:** Organizations face thousands of vulnerabilities identified by scanners, and the standard CVSS score alone is often insufficient for effective prioritization. AI provides a more context-aware risk score by enriching vulnerability data with crucial environmental factors: **Asset Criticality** (is the vulnerable system hosting critical data or supporting a key business service? Info from CMDB), **Threat Context** (is there known active exploitation of this vulnerability in the wild? Is there public exploit code available? Info from Threat Intelligence Platforms - TIPs), and **Network Exposure** (is the vulnerable system internet-facing? Can it be reached from less trusted network zones? Info from network topology/scans). AI combines these factors to highlight the vulnerabilities that pose the *actual greatest risk* to the *specific organization*, allowing teams to focus remediation efforts where they matter most.

- **Implementation Strategy:** Requires integrating data from multiple sources into a vulnerability management or security analytics platform: vulnerability scanner results (e.g., Qualys, Tenable, Rapid7), asset inventory/CMDB (including criticality tagging), threat intelligence feeds (mentioning specific CVEs being exploited), and potentially network topology or firewall rule analysis data. Develop or utilize an AI risk scoring engine (often using machine learning models or configurable weighting formulas) to calculate the contextualized risk score for each vulnerability instance. Prioritize remediation workflows based on this score.

- **Pain Points Addressed:** "Vulnerability overload" - too many vulnerabilities to patch with limited resources. Patching efforts diluted by focusing on technically severe (high CVSS) but low-risk vulnerabilities (e.g., on isolated, non-critical systems). Missing the truly critical vulnerabilities that are actively exploited and impact key assets. Difficulty demonstrating risk reduction to leadership.

- **Key AI Capability: Risk Scoring Models, Data Integration/Correlation, Graph Analysis** (optional, for network path analysis), **Threat Intelligence Correlation**.

- **Savings/Pros:** Focuses limited patching resources on the vulnerabilities most likely to be exploited and cause damage (Est: 60-80% reduction in critical vuln noise requiring immediate attention). Enables faster remediation of the highest actual risks, shrinking the window of exposure. Provides a more realistic and defensible view of vulnerability risk posture. Improves efficiency of vulnerability management teams.

- **Cons:** Highly dependent on the accuracy and completeness of input data, especially asset criticality from the CMDB and timely threat intelligence. Defining asset criticality consistently across the organization can be challenging. Risk scoring models require careful tuning and validation to align with organizational risk appetite.

54. Threat Hunting Hypothesis Generation & Validation

- **Explanation:** Proactive threat hunting involves searching for signs of undetected attackers within the environment, often starting with a hypothesis (e.g., "Are attackers using PowerShell for lateral movement?", "Is there C&C traffic disguised as DNS?"). AI assists hunters by automatically analyzing vast amounts of security data (logs, network flows, endpoint activity) and mapping observed patterns to known attacker tactics, techniques, and procedures (TTPs), often using frameworks like MITRE ATT&CK. Based on this analysis, AI can generate high-probability hypotheses about potential TTPs being used in *this specific environment* that warrant investigation, guiding hunters towards fruitful areas. It can also help quickly query data sources to validate or refute hypotheses.

- **Implementation Strategy:** Requires a powerful security analytics platform (e.g., advanced SIEM, XDR, data lake) capable of ingesting and correlating diverse security data at scale. Use AI techniques like pattern discovery, anomaly detection, clustering, graph analysis, and machine learning models trained to recognize specific TTPs or sequences of actions aligned with MITRE ATT&CK. The AI engine suggests hypotheses (e.g., "Potential lateral movement using WMI detected between servers X and Y") with supporting evidence (relevant log snippets, flow records) for analyst review and deeper investigation.
- **Pain Points Addressed:** Threat hunting often relies heavily on scarce expert intuition or follows generic industry reports, potentially missing environment-specific threats. Knowing where to start looking ("needle in a haystack" problem). Manually sifting through data to validate hypotheses is time-consuming.
- **Key AI Capability: Pattern Discovery, Correlation, Graph Analysis, Machine Learning (TTP Recognition/Mapping), MITRE ATT&CK Framework Integration.**
- **Savings/Pros:** Makes threat hunting more efficient and effective by providing data-driven starting points. Increases the chances of discovering novel or stealthy attacks missed by automated detection tools. Helps hunters prioritize their efforts based on observed activities. Systematizes the hunting process by leveraging frameworks like ATT&CK. Improves understanding of attacker behavior within the environment.
- **Cons:** Generated hypotheses still require significant investigation and validation by skilled human analysts. The quality of hypotheses depends heavily on the breadth and depth of data collected and the sophistication of the AI models. Can be computationally intensive. Requires analysts trained in threat hunting methodologies.

55. Automated Indicator of Compromise (IOC) Enrichment & Correlation

- **Explanation:** When a potential Indicator of Compromise (IOC) - like a suspicious IP address, domain name, file hash, or registry key - is identified (from threat feeds, alerts, or manual investigation), AI automates the tedious process of gathering context about it. It automatically queries multiple internal and external sources: **Threat Intelligence Platforms (TIPs)** (Is this IOC known bad? Associated malware families? Attacker groups?), **internal log databases** (Have we seen this IP/domain/hash in our environment before? When? Where?), **CMDB/asset inventory** (Which assets communicated with this IP? Which assets have this file hash?), and **vulnerability databases** (Are affected assets vulnerable to malware associated with this IOC?). This enriched context is presented synthesized to the analyst, drastically speeding up assessment and decision-making.
- **Implementation Strategy:** Typically implemented within a SOAR (Security Orchestration, Automation, and Response), TIP, or advanced SIEM platform. Requires configuring integrations (via APIs) with relevant internal systems (SIEM/log management, CMDB, vulnerability scanner) and external threat intelligence feeds (commercial or open

source). Define automated workflows (playbooks) that trigger upon IOC ingestion, query these sources in parallel, parse the results (using NLP where needed for reports), and aggregate the findings into a consolidated view within the alert or incident ticket.

- **Pain Points Addressed:** Manual research on individual IOCs is extremely time-consuming and repetitive for SOC analysts. Context gathering often involves querying multiple disconnected tools. Delays in understanding the relevance and scope of an IOC hinder rapid response.
- **Key AI Capability: Threat Intelligence Integration, Workflow Automation, Data Correlation/Aggregation, API Integration,** optional **NLP** (parsing unstructured threat reports).
- **Savings/Pros:** Dramatically reduces the time analysts spend manually researching IOCs (Est: 90%+ automated enrichment). Enables faster determination of whether an IOC represents a real threat to the organization. Provides immediate context on the potential scope of compromise (which assets involved). Allows analysts to focus on higher-level analysis and response actions. Improves consistency of investigation process.
- **Cons:** Effectiveness relies heavily on the quality, timeliness, and coverage of the integrated threat intelligence feeds and internal data sources. API integration with multiple tools can be complex to set up and maintain. Some context might still require manual interpretation (e.g., evaluating conflicting TI reports).

56.Security Playbook Recommendation & Automation (SOAR)

- **Explanation:** Security Orchestration, Automation, and Response (SOAR) platforms allow organizations to define standardized workflows ("playbooks") for responding to specific types of security incidents (e.g., phishing email reported, malware detected on endpoint, brute force login attempt). AI enhances SOAR by: 1) **Recommending** the most appropriate playbook based on the incoming alert's characteristics (type, severity, affected asset) using classification or case-based reasoning. 2) **Automating** the execution of predefined steps within the chosen playbook, such as: enriching data (like 6.5), creating tickets, blocking malicious IPs on firewalls, isolating infected endpoints via EDR tools, disabling user accounts, or triggering analyst notifications for specific decision points.
- **Implementation Strategy:** Requires deploying a SOAR platform and integrating it tightly with detection tools (SIEM, EDR, SEG), enrichment sources (TIP, CMDB), and response tools (firewall management, EDR, Active Directory). Define detailed response playbooks for common incident types. Implement AI classification models (trained on incident types and corresponding playbooks) for recommendation. Configure specific automation actions within playbooks, ensuring appropriate safeguards and human approval steps where necessary.
- **Pain Points Addressed:** Inconsistent incident response processes across different analysts or shifts. Slow manual execution of repetitive response tasks (blocking IPs, isolating hosts). Delays in containment leading to wider compromise. Overburdened SOC analysts spending time on low-level actions.

- **Key AI Capability: Classification/Case-Based Reasoning** (recommending playbooks), **Workflow Automation/Orchestration, API Integration**.
- **Savings/Pros:** Ensures consistent, best-practice response actions are followed for common incidents. Dramatically speeds up response times, especially containment actions (Est: 30-50% faster playbook execution). Reduces manual toil for SOC analysts, freeing them for complex investigations. Improves auditability of response actions. Enables 24/7 automated response capabilities for certain incident types.
- **Cons:** Requires significant initial investment in defining, building, and testing robust playbooks. Automation carries inherent risks - a flawed playbook action (e.g., blocking the wrong IP, isolating a critical server) can cause significant business disruption. Requires mature incident response processes as a foundation. Maintaining integrations with numerous tools can be complex.

57. Cloud Security Posture Management (CSPM) Anomaly Detection

- **Explanation:** Cloud environments are highly dynamic, and misconfigurations are a major source of breaches (e.g., public S3 buckets, overly permissive security group rules, weak IAM policies). AI enhances Cloud Security Posture Management (CSPM) by going beyond static rule checks. It learns the normal configuration patterns and activity within the cloud environment and detects anomalous changes or configurations that, while perhaps not violating a specific predefined rule, represent a significant deviation or potential risk. Examples include unusual permission escalations, security groups suddenly made open to the internet, or unexpected cross-account access patterns.
- **Implementation Strategy:** Integrate an AI-enabled CSPM tool or security analytics platform with cloud provider APIs (AWS Config, Azure Security Center, GCP Security Command Center) to continuously ingest configuration state data and activity logs. Establish baseline configurations and expected behavior patterns using AI (anomaly detection, clustering). Define policies based on security best practices. Use AI to detect deviations from baselines, violations of policies, or statistically anomalous configurations/activities. Generate prioritized alerts for the cloud security team or trigger automated remediation actions (with caution).
- **Pain Points Addressed:** Difficulty maintaining secure configurations in complex, rapidly changing cloud environments. Misconfigurations often go unnoticed until an audit or breach. Manual auditing is too slow and infrequent. Static policy checks can miss novel or context-specific risks.
- **Key AI Capability: Anomaly Detection** (config drift, unusual activity), **Policy Engines, Configuration Analysis, Cloud API Integration**.
- **Savings/Pros:** Enables proactive detection and remediation of risky cloud misconfigurations *before* they can be exploited. Provides continuous compliance monitoring against security best practices and internal policies. Reduces the likelihood of cloud breaches caused by configuration errors. Improves visibility and governance over dynamic cloud environments.

- **Cons:** Can generate noise if baselines are not well-established or if legitimate changes trigger alerts. Requires deep understanding of cloud service configurations and security best practices to configure effectively. Automated remediation of cloud configurations is particularly risky and requires extreme care.

58. AI-Assisted Malware Analysis (Static/Dynamic)

- **Explanation:** Manually analyzing suspicious files to determine if they are malicious (and if so, what they do) is a highly specialized and time-consuming task. AI assists malware analysts by automating parts of this process. **Static analysis** uses machine learning to rapidly classify files based on features extracted without running the code (e.g., strings, imported functions, code structure), often identifying known malware families or flagging suspicious characteristics. **Dynamic analysis** involves running the malware in a safe, instrumented environment (sandbox) and using AI to analyze its observed behavior (network connections, file system changes, registry modifications, processes launched), classify the behavior, and generate summarized reports identifying malicious actions and potential indicators of compromise (IOCs).
- **Implementation Strategy:** Integrate AI malware analysis engines (often cloud-based or on-prem appliances) with endpoint security (EDR), email security (SEG), or SOC workflows (e.g., submit suspicious files via SOAR). Use machine learning models (e.g., deep learning on byte sequences, gradient boosting on extracted features) trained on massive datasets of known goodware and malware. For dynamic analysis, utilize sandboxing technology coupled with AI behavior analysis. Results (classification score, detected behaviors, extracted IOCs) are fed back to analysts or used to trigger automated response actions.
- **Pain Points Addressed:** Malware analysis requires specialized reverse engineering skills which are scarce. Manual analysis is too slow to handle the high volume of suspicious files encountered daily. Difficulty quickly identifying known threats vs. novel ones requiring deeper investigation.
- **Key AI Capability: Classification** (malicious vs. benign, malware family), **Behavioral Analysis** (interpreting sandbox activity), **Machine Learning** (various types), **Feature Extraction**.
- **Savings/Pros:** Dramatically accelerates the initial triage and classification of suspicious files. Quickly identifies known malware, allowing analysts to focus scarce resources on unknown or highly sophisticated threats. Provides summarized behavioral reports and extracts potential IOCs automatically, speeding up incident response. Can handle much larger volumes than manual analysis alone.
- **Cons:** Advanced malware increasingly uses evasion techniques specifically designed to fool sandboxes and AI analysis (e.g., detecting virtualization, delaying malicious activity). AI analysis is generally not a replacement for expert human reverse engineering for truly complex or targeted malware. Accuracy depends heavily on the quality and diversity of the training data.

59. Adaptive Deception Technology Deployment

- **Explanation:** Deception technology uses decoys (honeypots, honeytokens, fake credentials) to lure attackers, detect their presence early, and gather intelligence on their TTPs. AI makes deception *adaptive*. Instead of static decoys that might become known or easily identifiable, AI analyzes attacker interactions with existing decoys (or general network threat activity) and dynamically modifies the decoys (e.g., changing OS appearance, open ports, types of fake data, lure documents) to make them more attractive, believable, and relevant to the specific attackers currently perceived in the environment. This increases the likelihood of engagement and improves the quality of intelligence gathered.
- **Implementation Strategy:** Requires deploying a sophisticated deception platform that supports dynamic modification of decoys via API. Integrate the platform with security analytics or threat intelligence feeds. Use AI algorithms (potentially reinforcement learning, or rule-based adaptation based on observed TTPs) to analyze attacker activity and determine optimal adjustments to decoy profiles. Orchestrate the automated reconfiguration of decoys based on AI recommendations. Monitor engagement with adapted decoys.
- **Pain Points Addressed:** Static honeypots can be fingerprinted and avoided by knowledgeable attackers. Decoys may not be relevant or attractive to the specific TTPs used in a current campaign. Difficulty manually updating and managing a large-scale deception environment.
- **Key AI Capability: Reinforcement Learning** (learning optimal decoy configurations), **Behavioral Analysis** (understanding attacker interactions), **Automation/Orchestration** (reconfiguring decoys), **Threat Intelligence Correlation**.
- **Savings/Pros:** Increases the effectiveness of deception technology by making it harder for attackers to identify and avoid. Gathers higher fidelity intelligence on active attacker TTPs specific to the environment. Can potentially steer attackers towards specific decoys for better monitoring or containment. Improves early detection capabilities for lateral movement and reconnaissance.
- **Cons:** High implementation complexity, requiring advanced deception platforms and AI integration. Potential risk that adaptation logic could be flawed or make decoys less effective. Careful design needed to ensure decoys remain distinguishable from real assets for defenders but not for attackers. Requires ongoing monitoring and analysis of attacker interactions.

60. Predictive Security Incident Escalation

- **Explanation:** SOCs often have tiered structures (L1, L2, L3 analysts). Determining when an alert or initial finding warrants escalation from a junior analyst (L1) to a more senior investigator (L2/L3) or the formal Incident Response (IR) team can be subjective. AI assists by analyzing multiple factors associated with an alert or developing situation -

the type and severity of the alert(s), the criticality of the involved asset(s), the risk score of the user(s) involved (from UEBA), correlation with other suspicious events, and comparison to historical patterns of major incidents - to predict the likelihood that this event requires escalation.

- **Implementation Strategy:** Integrate alert/event data from SIEM/detection tools with contextual data sources (CMDB, UEBA, TIP). Develop AI classification or risk scoring models trained on historical incident data, where past escalations (and their justifications) are labeled. The model outputs a probability score or classification (e.g., "High Likelihood of Escalation Needed"). This prediction can be used to automatically flag events for review by senior staff, adjust ticket priority, or trigger automated notifications to the appropriate escalation point.
- **Pain Points Addressed:** Inconsistent escalation decisions based on individual analyst experience or workload. Critical incidents being missed or delayed in escalation, allowing impact to grow. Senior analysts wasting time reviewing low-priority events unnecessarily escalated. Lack of clear, data-driven criteria for escalation.
- **Key AI Capability: Classification, Risk Scoring Models, Data Correlation, Predictive Analytics.**
- **Savings/Pros:** Ensures more consistent and timely escalation of potentially critical security incidents, enabling faster engagement by senior responders. Optimizes the workload distribution between SOC tiers, allowing L1 analysts to handle routine events and L2/L3 to focus on complex threats. Reduces the risk of major incidents being overlooked initially. Provides data-driven justification for escalation decisions.
- **Cons:** Accuracy depends heavily on the quality and labeling of historical incident data used for training. Requires careful definition of what constitutes a situation warranting escalation. Potential for false positives (flagging non-critical events) or false negatives (missing critical ones) requires ongoing monitoring and model tuning. Still requires human judgment, especially in ambiguous situations.

Chapter 8. Category 7: Incident Management & Resolution (ITSM/MIM) (Use Cases)

61.AI-Driven Event Correlation & Deduplication (MoM)

- **Explanation:** Modern IT environments generate a flood of events and alerts from numerous monitoring tools (infrastructure, network, APM, logs, cloud). An "alert storm" occurs when a single underlying issue (e.g., network switch failure) triggers dozens or hundreds of related alerts from dependent systems. AI acts as a "Manager of Managers" (MoM) by ingesting this raw event stream and intelligently correlating related events based on time proximity, topological relationships (understanding which systems depend on others using CMDB/discovery data), and textual similarity (using NLP on alert descriptions). It groups these related events into a single, consolidated incident and suppresses the redundant noise, providing Ops teams with a much clearer, actionable picture.
- **Implementation Strategy:** Requires centralizing all events/alerts from disparate monitoring tools into an AIOps platform. Ensure the platform has access to accurate topology information (from CMDB or discovery tools like 1.7). Utilize the platform's AI correlation engine, which employs algorithms like time-based clustering, graph-based correlation (following dependencies), and NLP-based similarity matching. Configure rules for incident creation based on correlated event clusters.
- **Pain Points Addressed:** Operations teams completely overwhelmed by the sheer volume of raw alerts ("alert fatigue"). Difficulty understanding the scope and origin of an issue amidst hundreds of symptomatic alerts. Multiple engineers potentially investigating different symptoms of the same root cause, wasting effort. Slow incident detection and diagnosis due to noise.
- **Key AI Capability: Clustering** (grouping related events), **Topology Analysis** (using dependencies for correlation), **NLP** (comparing alert messages), **Time-Series Correlation, Noise Reduction**.
- **Savings/Pros:** Achieves a massive reduction in the number of actionable items presented to operations (Est: 70-90% noise reduction is common). Provides a consolidated, contextualized view of incidents rather than isolated alerts. Significantly speeds up incident detection and initial triage. Reduces redundant investigation efforts. Improves situational awareness during outages.
- **Cons:** High implementation complexity, requiring robust integration of all monitoring tools and accurate topology data (often the biggest challenge). Correlation algorithms need careful tuning to avoid over-correlation (grouping unrelated events) or under-correlation (missing related events). Requires investment in a capable AIOps platform.

62. Intelligent Incident Ticket Classification & Routing

- **Explanation:** When users manually create tickets via a portal or email, or when basic monitoring tools generate generic tickets, they often lack proper categorization or assignment. AI uses Natural Language Processing (NLP) to read the ticket's subject line and description, understand the user's intent or the nature of the reported issue (e.g., "network slow," "password reset required," "database error"), automatically classify the ticket into the correct category (e.g., Network, Security, Database, End User Compute), and route it to the appropriate support team's queue within the IT Service Management (ITSM) tool.

- **Implementation Strategy:** Integrate an AI engine (often built-in or add-on to modern ITSM platforms like ServiceNow, BMC Helix, Jira Service Management) with the ticketing system. Train NLP classification models using historical ticket data (descriptions correlated with their manually assigned categories and resolution groups). Configure the ITSM workflow to pass new ticket descriptions to the AI for automatic population of the 'Category', 'Subcategory', and 'Assignment Group' fields. Continuously refine the model based on user feedback or manual corrections.

- **Pain Points Addressed:** Tickets routed to the wrong team ("ticket ping-pong"), causing significant delays in starting resolution work. Manual triage of incoming tickets by Service Desk or L1 teams consumes valuable time. Inconsistent categorization impacts reporting and trend analysis. User frustration due to slow response times caused by mis-routing.

- **Key AI Capability: Natural Language Processing (NLP), Text Classification, Machine Learning.**

- **Savings/Pros:** Significantly accelerates the time it takes for a ticket to reach the correct resolvers (Est: 90%+ routing accuracy achievable). Reduces overall Mean Time To Resolution (MTTR) by eliminating routing delays. Decreases the manual workload on Service Desk / L1 teams performing triage. Improves consistency of ticket categorization for better reporting and analysis.

- **Cons:** Requires a substantial volume of clean, well-categorized historical ticket data for effective model training. Ambiguous or poorly written ticket descriptions can still lead to misclassification. Models need ongoing retraining to adapt to new services, terminology, or issue types.

63. Automated Incident Prioritization Based on Business Impact

- **Explanation:** Traditional incident priority is often based on technical urgency (e.g., P1 for server down) or impact (number of users affected). AI provides a more business-aware prioritization by automatically determining the *business services* supported by the affected Configuration Item (CI) using data from the CMDB. It can then assign priority based on the criticality of those business services (e.g., revenue-generating platform vs. internal tool), potential financial impact, SLA commitments, or even the time of day (e.g., issue during peak business hours). This ensures IT focuses effort on incidents with the highest actual or potential business impact.

- **Implementation Strategy:** Requires a relatively mature and accurate CMDB that maps technical CIs (servers, applications, databases, network devices) to the business services they support, along with criticality attributes assigned to those business services. Integrate the ITSM tool with the CMDB. Use AI (graph analysis to traverse dependencies, rule engines applying business logic, or classification models) to calculate a business impact score when an incident affects a CI. Configure ITSM workflows to set the incident priority based on this calculated score, potentially overriding default technical priorities.
- **Pain Points Addressed:** IT teams spending urgent effort fixing issues that have minimal impact on core business functions, while truly critical business services remain degraded. Difficulty aligning IT priorities with business priorities during incident management. Inconsistent priority setting based on subjective judgment. Poor communication of business impact to stakeholders.
- **Key AI Capability: Graph Analysis** (CMDB traversal), **Rule Engines, Classification, Risk Scoring, Data Enrichment.**
- **Savings/Pros:** Ensures IT resources are focused on resolving incidents that matter most to the business bottom line. Reduces the business impact duration and cost of outages. Improves alignment and communication between IT and business stakeholders. Provides a more objective and consistent method for setting incident priorities. Helps meet business-level SLAs more effectively.
- **Cons:** Critically dependent on the existence, accuracy, and completeness of the CMDB, including the crucial mapping between CIs and business services (this is often a major organizational challenge). Defining business criticality objectively can be difficult. Rules for calculating impact need careful design and consensus.

64. Root Cause Analysis Candidate Suggestion

- **Explanation:** Once an incident is detected and correlated (by 7.1), AI analyzes the associated data - correlated alerts, details of affected CIs, recent configuration changes in the vicinity (from change management records), anomalous log patterns (from 1.3), performance metric deviations, and topological dependencies - to suggest a ranked list of the most statistically likely root causes. It might also leverage knowledge from past similar incidents (using 7.6). This guides the troubleshooting efforts of human responders, helping them focus on the most probable culprits first.
- **Implementation Strategy:** Within an AIOps or advanced ITSM platform, feed all relevant contextual data surrounding a correlated incident into AI models. These models might use probabilistic methods (Bayesian inference), advanced correlation techniques, graph algorithms tracing impact paths backwards, or case-based reasoning comparing the current incident's "symptom fingerprint" to past incidents. Present the top N likely root cause candidates (e.g., "Recent change CHG12345 on firewall FW-01," "High database CPU on DBServer05," "Network latency spike on link X") directly within the incident view.

- **Pain Points Addressed:** Incident responders wasting valuable time exploring incorrect hypotheses or chasing symptoms instead of the true root cause. "War rooms" getting stuck due to lack of clear direction. Slow Mean Time To Identify (MTTI) / Root Cause Identification (RCI). Difficulty correlating disparate pieces of information manually under pressure.
- **Key AI Capability: Correlation Engines, Probabilistic Modeling (e.g., Bayesian Networks), Case-Based Reasoning, Graph Analysis, Change Correlation**.
- **Savings/Pros:** Significantly accelerates root cause identification (Est: Top 3 suggestions often include the actual RC >70% of the time in mature systems), leading to faster MTTR. Reduces wasted troubleshooting effort. Provides data-driven starting points for investigation. Helps less experienced staff by suggesting likely paths. Captures and reuses knowledge from past incidents.
- **Cons:** Suggestions are probabilistic hypotheses, not definitive answers; human expertise is still required for confirmation. Accuracy depends heavily on the quality, completeness, and timeliness of the ingested contextual data (especially change records and topology). Complex, novel, or multi-faceted incidents can still be challenging for AI to diagnose.

65.Automated Diagnostic Data Collection for Incidents

- **Explanation:** When an incident occurs, engineers often need specific diagnostic data (e.g., thread dumps from an application server, detailed performance counters from a database, specific log files from relevant time window, network packet captures) to troubleshoot effectively. AI/automation can automatically trigger the collection of this data based on the type of incident, the affected CI(s), or initial analysis findings. This ensures the necessary data is captured promptly (before conditions change or logs roll over) and made readily available to the resolvers, eliminating manual fetching delays.
- **Implementation Strategy:** Define standard diagnostic procedures and required data points for different types of CIs or common incident scenarios (e.g., "For Application X crash, get thread dump, heap dump, and last 10 mins of app logs"). Develop scripts or automation workflows (using SOAR, Runbook Automation tools, or agent-based capabilities) to execute these data collection tasks remotely on the target systems. Integrate the automation platform with the ITSM/AIOps tool so that incident creation or specific triggers (e.g., AI suggesting a likely root cause) automatically initiate the relevant data collection playbook. Store collected data centrally (e.g., attached to the incident ticket, in a shared drive).
- **Pain Points Addressed:** Delays in incident resolution while engineers manually log into systems to collect logs or diagnostic files. Inconsistent data collection steps followed by different engineers. Critical data being lost (e.g., logs overwritten, state changed) before it can be captured manually. Repetitive, low-value task for skilled engineers.
- **Key AI Capability: Workflow Automation, Scripting/RPA, Integration (ITSM/AIOps to Automation Tools)**, optional **NLP** (interpreting requests for specific data).
- **Savings/Pros:** Ensures diagnostic data is available much faster (Est: 50-70% faster acquisition), reducing MTTR. Guarantees consistency in the type and format of data

collected. Captures data closer to the time of the event, increasing relevance. Frees up resolver time to focus on analysis rather than data gathering. Reduces errors associated with manual collection.

- **Cons:** Requires pre-defining diagnostic procedures and developing robust automation scripts for various scenarios and system types. Need secure mechanisms and credentials for the automation platform to access target systems. Scripts need maintenance as systems or diagnostic commands change. Storing large diagnostic files requires adequate infrastructure.

66.Similar Incident Matching & Resolution Recommendation

- **Explanation:** Many IT incidents are recurring. AI uses NLP and machine learning (vector embeddings, similarity algorithms) to analyze the description, classification, affected CI, and other attributes of a *new* incident and automatically search through the historical incident database and potentially the Knowledge Base (KB). It identifies past incidents or KB articles that are highly similar in nature and presents their documented resolutions, workarounds, or related information directly to the engineer working on the current ticket.

- **Implementation Strategy:** Requires indexing the content (descriptions, resolution notes, keywords) of historical incident tickets and KB articles within the ITSM tool or a dedicated AI search engine. Use AI techniques like NLP (to understand semantics beyond keywords) and vector similarity search (to find conceptually similar text even if wording differs). Integrate the similarity search results directly into the incident ticket interface, presenting the most relevant past incidents/articles with links.

- **Pain Points Addressed:** Engineers frequently "reinventing the wheel" by troubleshooting issues that have been solved before. Knowledge trapped in poorly indexed historical tickets or not documented in the KB. Inconsistent resolutions applied to similar problems by different engineers. Slow resolution for recurring issues due to lack of readily available known fixes.

- **Key AI Capability: Natural Language Processing (NLP), Vector Search/Similarity Algorithms, Recommendation Engines, Information Retrieval.**

- **Savings/Pros:** Significantly speeds up resolution for recurring incidents by providing proven fixes immediately (Est: Find relevant past resolutions >80% of the time). Improves the consistency and quality of resolutions. Promotes knowledge reuse and reduces reliance on individual heroics. Helps identify gaps where recurring issues should be documented in the KB. Can onboard new staff faster by providing relevant historical context.

- **Cons:** Effectiveness is highly dependent on the quality, consistency, and completeness of descriptions and resolution notes in historical tickets ("Garbage In, Garbage Out"). Requires a sufficiently large historical dataset. Similarity matching can sometimes return irrelevant results, requiring filtering by the engineer. Needs ongoing indexing and model refinement.

67. Major Incident (MIM) Prediction & Early Warning

- **Explanation:** Major Incidents (P1/Severe) require dedicated management processes (Major Incident Management - MIM) and rapid mobilization. AI analyzes the characteristics of newly emerging or developing incidents - considering factors like the rate of incoming correlated alerts, the criticality of the initially affected CIs (based on 7.3), keywords in alerts/tickets suggesting widespread impact ("outage," "unavailable," "multiple users"), unusual patterns detected by anomaly detection (1.2, 1.3), or similarity to past major incidents - to predict if an incident has a high probability of escalating into a full-blown Major Incident *before* it formally meets the strict MIM criteria (e.g., number of users impacted, duration). This provides an early warning to MIM managers and key stakeholders.
- **Implementation Strategy:** Feed data about newly created/correlated incidents, including alert velocity, CI criticality, textual content, and anomaly flags from AIOps tooling, into AI classification or risk scoring models. Train these models on historical data, labeling incidents that eventually became Major Incidents. Generate high-priority alerts or notifications specifically tagged as "Potential Major Incident" when the AI prediction exceeds a defined confidence threshold. Route these early warnings to the on-call MIM team or relevant leadership.
- **Pain Points Addressed:** Major Incidents are often declared too late, after significant business impact has already occurred and spread. Reactive engagement of MIM processes and resources delays coordinated response. Difficulty distinguishing potentially severe incidents from routine ones in the early stages.
- **Key AI Capability: Classification, Anomaly Detection, Risk Scoring, Predictive Analytics, NLP** (keyword spotting).
- **Savings/Pros:** Enables proactive mobilization of the Major Incident Management team and necessary resources *before* the situation fully escalates. Potentially allows for faster containment or mitigation actions, reducing the overall duration and impact of major outages. Improves situational awareness for leadership early on. Streamlines the decision process for formal MIM declaration.
- **Cons:** Potential for false positives - predicting a Major Incident that doesn't materialize - which could lead to unnecessary resource mobilization or "cry wolf" syndrome if too frequent. Requires well-defined characteristics of past Major Incidents and their precursors for effective training. Model tuning is critical to balance sensitivity and specificity.

68. Automated MIM Communication Drafting & Stakeholder Updates

- **Explanation:** During a high-pressure Major Incident, the Incident Commander or Communications Manager spends critical time drafting status updates for various audiences (technical teams needing details, executives needing impact summaries, end-users needing awareness). AI assists by automatically generating draft communications based on structured data already available in the incident record (e.g., affected service, business impact assessment from 7.3, identified root cause candidates from 7.4, key resolution steps being taken, estimated time to resolution - ETR). The AI uses templates and NLP generation to create audience-appropriate drafts, which the manager can quickly review, edit, and send.

- **Implementation Strategy:** Integrate an AI text generation engine (potentially fine-tuned on past incident communications or using customizable templates) with the ITSM/MIM tool. Define templates for different audiences and communication types (initial alert, update, resolution). Configure workflows to automatically trigger draft generation when key incident fields are updated (e.g., ETR changed, workaround identified). Populate templates with real-time incident data via API calls. Ensure drafts are clearly marked and require human review and approval before being sent through integrated communication channels (email, status pages, chat platforms).
- **Pain Points Addressed:** Incident Commanders getting bogged down writing communications instead of managing the resolution effort. Delays in sending out critical updates to stakeholders. Inconsistent messaging quality, tone, or level of detail across different updates or incidents. Risk of errors in manually compiled updates.
- **Key AI Capability: NLP (Text Generation), Workflow Automation, Template Management, Data Integration**.
- **Savings/Pros:** Significantly reduces the time and effort required to draft incident communications (Est: 60-80% faster drafting). Ensures faster, more frequent, and consistent updates to all stakeholders. Improves stakeholder satisfaction and manages expectations better. Frees up the Incident Commander to focus on driving resolution. Reduces errors in communications.
- **Cons:** Generated text absolutely requires human review and editing for accuracy, tone, context, and political sensitivity before sending. Effectiveness depends heavily on the quality and timeliness of structured data being entered into the incident record. NLP models need careful design and training/tuning to produce appropriate output. Over-reliance could lead to impersonal or inaccurate messages if not managed well.

69.AI-Assisted Post-Incident Review (PIR) Data Gathering & Analysis

- **Explanation:** Conducting thorough Post-Incident Reviews (PIRs) or Post-Mortems is crucial for learning and preventing recurrence, but manually gathering all the relevant data and compiling the report is tedious. AI automates much of the data gathering by pulling together the complete incident timeline (from ITSM), correlated alerts and metrics (from AIOps), relevant configuration changes made before or during the incident (from change management), key decisions or conversations (potentially from linked chat logs like Slack/Teams using NLP), and resolution steps taken. It can then summarize key event sequences, highlight deviations from normal performance, and potentially even suggest contributing factors or areas for follow-up actions based on patterns or comparison to best practices.
- **Implementation Strategy:** Requires an integrated tools environment where the AIOps/ITSM platform can access data from monitoring tools, change management

systems, and potentially collaboration platforms via APIs. Use AI correlation, NLP (for summarizing text logs/chats), and timeline generation algorithms to automatically assemble a draft PIR document or data repository. Identify key metrics deviations, configuration changes coinciding with the incident, and potentially compare the incident pattern to known anti-patterns or previous PIR recommendations. Present the collated data and AI-generated insights for human review and finalization.

- **Pain Points Addressed:** PIRs are often delayed, incomplete, or skipped entirely due to the significant manual effort required to collect data and write the report. Subjectivity and bias can creep into manually constructed timelines or analyses. Key insights are often missed due to information overload or lack of correlation. Difficulty tracking follow-up actions.
- **Key AI Capability: NLP (Summarization, Timeline Extraction), Correlation, Data Aggregation, Pattern Recognition, Change Impact Analysis.**
- **Savings/Pros:** Dramatically reduces the time and manual effort needed to prepare PIRs (Est: 50%+ time reduction). Provides a more objective, data-driven foundation for the review. Helps identify contributing factors and actionable follow-up items more effectively. Improves organizational learning from incidents. Facilitates faster completion and distribution of PIRs. Ensures consistency in PIR data gathering.
- **Cons:** AI analysis may miss subtle human factors, process issues, or contextual nuances that are critical to understanding the incident. Accessing and correlating data from diverse sources (especially chat logs) can be technically complex and raise privacy concerns. AI suggestions still require thorough review and interpretation by experienced personnel. The quality of the output depends on the quality of the input data recorded during the incident.

70. Predictive Incident SLA Breach Risk Assessment

- **Explanation:** AI predicts the likelihood that an *currently open* incident will fail to meet its defined Service Level Agreement (SLA) target for resolution time. It analyzes various factors: the incident's current priority, its complexity (based on category, CI type, or historical data), the current workload and historical performance of the assigned team or individual, the time elapsed so far, and comparison to the resolution times of statistically similar past incidents. This prediction provides an early warning to Service Level Managers or team leads, allowing them to proactively intervene (e.g., escalate, reassign, add resources) to prevent the potential breach.
- **Implementation Strategy:** Requires data from the ITSM tool including incident details (priority, category, assignment group, age), SLA definitions, team workload information (e.g., number of open tickets per assignee), and, crucially, historical incident resolution data. Train AI classification or regression models to predict breach likelihood (e.g., % probability) or estimate the final resolution time based on current state and historical patterns. Integrate the prediction output directly into incident dashboards or trigger automated alerts/notifications when breach risk exceeds a defined threshold.

- **Pain Points Addressed:** SLAs breached unexpectedly, impacting performance metrics, customer satisfaction, and potentially contractual obligations. Difficulty proactively identifying incidents that are falling behind schedule until it's too late. Inconsistent focus on at-risk incidents. Lack of data to support resource allocation decisions for preventing breaches.
- **Key AI Capability: Classification** (breach / no breach prediction), **Regression** (predicting resolution time), **Workload Analysis**, **Predictive Analytics**.
- **Savings/Pros:** Provides early warning of potential SLA failures, enabling proactive management intervention (Est: >75% of eventual breaches can often be predicted early). Helps prioritize focus on incidents most likely to breach. Improves overall SLA performance and compliance reporting. Provides data for justifying resource allocation or process improvements. Reduces penalties or reputational damage associated with SLA failures.
- **Cons:** Predictive accuracy depends heavily on the quality and volume of historical incident data and the predictability of incident resolution work (some incidents are inherently unpredictable). Requires accurate tracking of team workload and assignment. Models need to be retrained periodically to adapt to changing team performance or incident patterns. External factors (e.g., vendor delays) impacting resolution time can be hard to model.

Chapter 9. Category 8: Service Desk & End-User Experience (Use Cases)

71. Intelligent Chatbot/Virtual Agent for Tier 1 Support

- **Explanation:** An AI-powered chatbot, often integrated into platforms like Microsoft Teams, Slack, or a web portal, serves as the initial contact for end-users facing IT issues. Using Natural Language Processing (NLP) to understand user requests phrased in everyday language, it can autonomously resolve common Tier 1 problems. This includes executing automated password resets (via IAM integration), unlocking accounts, providing step-by-step troubleshooting guides for basic issues (e.g., printer connection, Wi-Fi access), answering frequently asked questions by querying the knowledge base, checking the status of existing support tickets, and intelligently logging a ticket with the correct categorization for issues requiring human intervention, ensuring a seamless handoff.

- **Implementation Strategy:** Requires deploying a chatbot platform (e.g., native ITSM capabilities, specialized tools like Kore.ai, Aisera, or cloud platforms like Dialogflow). Integrate tightly with the ITSM system (for ticket logging/status), Knowledge Base (for answering FAQs), Identity and Access Management (IAM) systems (for password/account actions), and potentially basic automation tools. Train the NLP model on typical user intents, entities (like application names), and company-specific jargon. Define clear conversational flows and robust escalation paths to human agents when the bot reaches its limits. Monitor interaction logs for continuous improvement and training.

- **Pain Points Addressed:** Service Desk overwhelmed by high volume of simple, repetitive L1 requests. Long user wait times for basic assistance (especially password resets), hindering productivity. High operational costs associated with 24/7 human L1 support coverage. Inconsistent answers provided by different agents for common questions.

- **Key AI Capability: Natural Language Processing (NLP), Dialogue Management, Intent Recognition, Entity Extraction, Knowledge Base Integration, Workflow Automation (via API calls).**

- **Savings/Pros:** Significant deflection of requests from human agents (Est: 30-50% or more of L1 volume), leading to reduced L1 support costs. Provides instant, 24/7 resolution for common issues, improving user satisfaction and reducing productivity loss. Ensures consistent, approved answers. Frees up human agents for more complex, engaging tasks. Scalable to handle demand peaks.

- **Cons:** Can frustrate users if NLP fails to understand intent or if conversation flows are poorly designed. Effectiveness heavily relies on a comprehensive and well-maintained Knowledge Base. Requires robust backend integration for automated actions (password reset, etc.). Continuous training and tuning are necessary. May struggle with nuanced or multi-part requests.

72. Predictive User Hardware Failure (Laptop Disk/Battery)

- **Explanation:** This leverages AI to shift from reactive to proactive endpoint hardware support. By analyzing telemetry data continuously collected by endpoint agents (e.g., from Intune, Workspace ONE, Tanium) - specifically focusing on hardware health indicators like S.M.A.R.T. stats for disk drives (predicting drive failure), battery charge cycles, maximum capacity degradation, cell voltage irregularities (predicting battery failure), and potentially anomalous crash dumps or performance metrics correlated with past hardware issues - AI models can predict imminent failures with a reasonable degree of accuracy. This allows IT to schedule a replacement *before* the user experiences a disruptive failure and downtime.
- **Implementation Strategy:** Deploy endpoint management agents capable of collecting detailed hardware telemetry. Establish a data pipeline to centralize this telemetry. Develop or utilize AI forecasting models (time-series analysis focusing on degradation trends, anomaly detection for sudden deviations) trained on historical failure data correlated with specific telemetry patterns. Set thresholds for predictive alerts. Integrate alerts with the ITSM system to automatically generate service requests for proactive device swaps or component replacements.
- **Pain Points Addressed:** Significant loss of user productivity and potential data loss when laptops fail unexpectedly (disk crash, battery failure). Reactive replacement process causes user disruption and often requires emergency shipping/support. Difficulty managing hardware lifecycle efficiently. User dissatisfaction from unreliable equipment.
- **Key AI Capability: Time-Series Forecasting, Anomaly Detection, Predictive Maintenance Modeling, Sensor Data Analysis (SMART, Battery chem).**
- **Savings/Pros:** Greatly reduces user downtime and associated productivity loss. Improves user satisfaction and confidence in IT equipment. Allows for planned, non-disruptive device replacements, optimizing logistics and support resources. Potentially extends usable device life by replacing components (like batteries) proactively instead of the whole device. Fewer emergency repairs/replacements needed. Helps optimize hardware refresh budgets.
- **Cons:** Requires robust endpoint agent deployment and management. Centralizing and managing large volumes of telemetry data can be demanding. Predictive accuracy varies depending on component type and available data (batteries are notoriously tricky). False positives can lead to unnecessary replacements (costly). Privacy implications of collecting detailed device data must be addressed.

73. Automated Software Request Fulfillment & Licensing Check

- **Explanation:** This automates the end-to-end process for users requesting standard, approved software titles. When a user initiates a request (via a service catalog portal, chatbot like 71, or perhaps even email parsing), AI/automation takes over. It first verifies the user's eligibility based on role, department, or existing permissions (querying AD/HR data). It then checks license availability within the license management system (like

2.9/19) to ensure compliance. If approval is needed, it triggers the appropriate workflow (e.g., manager approval via ITSM). Upon successful eligibility check, license validation, and approval, it automatically instructs the endpoint management system (SCCM, Intune, Jamf) to deploy the software package to the user's device and updates asset management and license allocation records accordingly.

- **Implementation Strategy:** Requires seamless API integration between the request intake channel (Service Catalog/ITSM portal, Chatbot), Identity Management (AD/IAM for eligibility), License Management tool, Approval Workflow engine (ITSM), and Software Deployment tools (UEM/Client Management). Utilize workflow automation platforms (RPA, SOAR, or native ITSM automation) governed by rule engines to orchestrate the process. Standardized software packages suitable for automated deployment are essential.
- **Pain Points Addressed:** Slow turnaround times for software requests, hindering user productivity ('Day 1 readiness' issues). Significant manual effort for Service Desk or Desktop Support teams handling fulfillment. Risk of installing unlicensed software or exceeding license counts, leading to compliance issues and financial penalties. Inconsistent application of eligibility or approval policies.
- **Key AI Capability: Workflow Automation/Orchestration**, **Rule Engines** (Eligibility, Licensing, Approval Logic), **API Integration**, **NLP** (optional, for parsing free-text requests).
- **Savings/Pros:** Dramatically faster software delivery to end-users (Est: 70-90% faster for standard titles achievable). Significant reduction in manual support effort. Ensures software license compliance automatically. Provides a consistent and auditable fulfillment process. Improves user satisfaction through speed and efficiency.
- **Cons:** Primarily suitable for standard, pre-packaged software titles. Requires significant initial setup effort to build integrations and workflows. Robust error handling within the automation is critical. Maintaining automated deployment packages requires ongoing effort. Complex licensing models might be difficult to automate checks for.

74.User Sentiment Analysis from Tickets, Surveys, Chat

- **Explanation:** This involves using AI, specifically Natural Language Processing (NLP), to automatically analyze the unstructured text feedback provided by users across various channels. This includes comments in ITSM tickets (incident descriptions, resolution confirmations), free-text responses in customer satisfaction (CSAT) surveys, and transcripts from interactions with chatbots or live agents. The AI identifies the emotional tone (positive, negative, neutral) - the sentiment - and can also perform topic modeling or keyword extraction to pinpoint the specific subjects users are discussing (e.g., "slow response," "knowledgeable agent," "website confusing," "password policy"). This provides richer insights than numerical ratings alone, highlighting *why* users feel a certain way and identifying recurring themes or emerging issues.
- **Implementation Strategy:** Collect and aggregate text feedback from ITSM, survey platforms, and chat logs. Utilize NLP services (cloud-based like Azure Text Analytics, AWS Comprehend, or integrated within ITSM/analytics tools) pre-trained for sentiment

analysis and topic modeling. Models may benefit from fine-tuning using company-specific examples. Integrate results into dashboards visualizing sentiment trends over time, comparing scores across services or support teams, and listing frequently mentioned positive/negative topics.

- **Pain Points Addressed:** Lack of understanding behind quantitative satisfaction scores (e.g., why is CSAT dropping?). Valuable qualitative feedback buried within large volumes of text comments, rarely analyzed systematically. Difficulty spotting emerging trends in user complaints or compliments quickly. Manual review of comments is subjective, time-consuming, and unscalable.
- **Key AI Capability: Natural Language Processing (NLP), Sentiment Analysis, Topic Modeling, Keyword Extraction.**
- **Savings/Pros:** Provides deep, actionable insights into the *drivers* of user satisfaction/dissatisfaction. Enables identification of specific process bottlenecks, service issues, or training needs for agents. Allows tracking the impact of improvement initiatives on user perception over time. Complements quantitative metrics for a holistic view of user experience. Facilitates data-driven prioritization of service improvements.
- **Cons:** Sentiment analysis accuracy can be imperfect, struggling with sarcasm, nuanced language, or mixed emotions within a single comment. Requires a sufficient volume of text data for meaningful trend analysis. Insights are only valuable if translated into concrete actions. May require some tuning for domain-specific (IT support) language. Privacy issues if analyzing potentially sensitive ticket details.

75. Proactive Outage Notification to Affected Users

- **Explanation:** Instead of waiting for users to report an outage, this leverages AI-driven monitoring (like Category 1 use cases) and automation to communicate proactively. When the monitoring system detects and confirms a service outage affecting specific Configuration Items (CIs - e.g., servers, applications, network devices), an automated workflow cross-references these CIs against the Configuration Management Database (CMDB). The CMDB relationship data allows the system to identify the business services impacted and, crucially, the specific users or departments who rely on those services. The system then automatically generates and sends targeted notifications (via email, SMS, Teams/Slack alert, status page update, portal banner) only to the *affected* user population, informing them of the issue, expected impact, and estimated resolution time (if known).
- **Implementation Strategy:** Requires tight integration between the event/incident management system (where confirmed outages are flagged), the CMDB (which must contain accurate mappings between CIs, Business Services, and Users/Departments), and communication tools/channels. Utilize workflow automation to trigger the notification process based on incident severity and CI impact. Templates ensure consistent messaging.
- **Pain Points Addressed:** Service Desk being flooded with redundant calls/tickets from users reporting an already known outage. User frustration and productivity loss due to

lack of timely information about service disruptions. Damage to IT credibility when users discover outages before IT communicates them. Inefficient broadcast communications hitting unaffected users.

- **Key AI Capability: Graph Analysis (CMDB Relationship Traversal)**, **Workflow Automation**, **Data Integration**.
- **Savings/Pros:** Dramatically reduces inbound call/ticket volume to the Service Desk during major incidents. Improves user experience and trust by providing timely, relevant information. Allows Service Desk agents to focus on gathering diagnostic info or supporting workaround efforts instead of answering repetitive calls. Faster dissemination of critical information. Reduces user frustration.
- **Cons:** Critically dependent on the accuracy and completeness of the CMDB, especially the mapping of CIs to business services and users/groups. Defining the trigger conditions and target audiences requires careful planning. Risk of sending incorrect or alarming notifications if CMDB data is wrong.

76. Enhanced Self-Service Password Reset (Voice/Behavior Biometrics)

- **Explanation:** Traditional Self-Service Password Reset (SSPR) often relies on security questions (Knowledge-Based Authentication - KBA), which can be forgotten by users or potentially compromised. This uses AI to introduce more secure and user-friendly multi-factor authentication options within the SSPR workflow. Examples include: **Voice Biometrics**, where the user speaks a passphrase and the AI verifies their unique voice print against a pre-enrolled sample; or **Behavioral Biometrics**, where the AI analyzes *how* a user types a known piece of information or interacts with the mouse, comparing patterns against their established baseline to verify identity implicitly. These methods can replace or supplement KBA.
- **Implementation Strategy:** Integrate a third-party biometric authentication provider (specializing in voice, behavioral, or other modalities) with the existing SSPR portal/tool via APIs. Requires an initial user enrollment process to capture the voice print or establish the behavioral baseline. During a reset attempt, the SSPR tool invokes the biometric provider's API for verification. The AI matching algorithms run within the provider's service.
- **Pain Points Addressed:** Password resets remain a very high-volume driver of calls to the Service Desk, even with basic SSPR. Users forgetting answers to security questions. Security risks associated with easily guessable or socially engineered KBA answers. Poor user experience with cumbersome KBA processes.
- **Key AI Capability: Biometric Analysis (Voice Recognition, Behavioral Pattern Matching)**, **Anomaly Detection** (detecting deviations from enrolled biometric templates), **Machine Learning Classification** (matching attempts).
- **Savings/Pros:** Potential for further significant reduction in password reset related calls to the Service Desk. Can offer stronger security assurance than KBA alone. Improves user convenience by replacing potentially forgotten questions with inherent factors (voice) or implicit actions (behavior). Modernizes the user authentication experience.

- **Cons:** User acceptance and privacy concerns related to collecting biometric data need careful management and clear communication. Requires an initial user enrollment step, which can be a hurdle. Accuracy of biometric systems is not 100% (false accepts/rejects possible, though rates are improving). Potential for sophisticated spoofing attacks exists, requiring robust anti-spoofing measures from the provider.

77.Personalized Knowledge Base Article Recommendations

- **Explanation:** This aims to make self-service via the Knowledge Base (KB) more effective. Instead of relying solely on keyword matching, AI provides smarter recommendations. When a user searches the KB, interacts with a chatbot (like 71), or even views an incident ticket, the AI considers multiple factors: the user's search query or issue description (using NLP for semantic understanding), the user's role, department, or location, their past ticket history or previously viewed articles, and potentially articles that were found helpful by other users with similar profiles or issues (collaborative filtering). Based on this context, it presents a ranked list of the most likely relevant KB articles.
- **Implementation Strategy:** Requires indexing the KB content (articles, guides, FAQs). Integrate an AI recommendation engine (using NLP, collaborative filtering, content-based filtering algorithms) with the KB search interface, chatbot platform, and potentially the ITSM agent view. Ensure user profile data and interaction history are available to the recommendation engine (respecting privacy). Continuously refine recommendations based on user feedback (clicks, ratings, resolution success).
- **Pain Points Addressed:** Users struggling to find the correct information in large, complex Knowledge Bases using basic keyword search. Low success rates for self-service attempts, leading users to contact the Service Desk unnecessarily. Relevant content exists but is hard to discover.
- **Key AI Capability: Natural Language Processing (NLP), Recommendation Engines (Collaborative Filtering, Content-Based Filtering), User Profiling, Information Retrieval**.
- **Savings/Pros:** Increases the likelihood of users successfully resolving issues via self-service, leading to greater ticket deflection. Reduces escalations to human agents. Provides faster answers and a better self-service experience for users. Helps surface the most relevant and effective KB content.
- **Cons:** Effectiveness heavily depends on the quality, structure, and comprehensiveness of the underlying Knowledge Base content. Requires sufficient usage data (searches, views, ticket links) for collaborative filtering models to become effective. May require investment in advanced search/recommendation tools or platforms. Maintaining user profile data accurately can be a challenge.

78.Optimized New Hire Onboarding Workflow Automation

- **Explanation:** Onboarding a new employee involves numerous tasks across multiple departments (HR, IT, Facilities, Finance) - creating accounts, assigning licenses, provisioning hardware, granting access to applications and network shares, setting up physical workspace, etc. This use case focuses on using AI and workflow automation to orchestrate and optimize this complex process. Based on the new hire's role, location, and start date (often sourced from the HR system), the automation platform automatically triggers the necessary tasks in the correct sequence, routes approvals electronically, and tracks progress. AI can potentially optimize task scheduling or handle variations based on learned patterns or defined rules, ensuring everything is ready for the employee's first day.

- **Implementation Strategy:** Requires detailed mapping of the end-to-end onboarding process across all involved departments. Utilize a robust workflow automation or Business Process Management (BPM) tool capable of integrating via API with key systems: HR system (source of truth for new hires), ITSM (for IT task tracking/approvals), Active Directory/IAM (account creation/access), Endpoint Management (device provisioning), Facilities Management systems, etc. Implement rule engines or potentially AI decision models to handle role-based variations and dependencies.

- **Pain Points Addressed:** Slow, manual, and often error-prone onboarding processes leading to delays in new hire productivity ('Day 1 readiness' failures). Inconsistent experience for new hires depending on manager or location. Significant administrative overhead and coordination effort across multiple teams. Lack of visibility into onboarding status.

- **Key AI Capability: Workflow Optimization, Process Automation (RPA/BPM), Rule Engines, API Integration**, potentially **Scheduling Optimization**.

- **Savings/Pros:** Significantly reduces the time required to onboard new employees, accelerating their time-to-productivity (Est: 30-50% faster overall process). Provides a consistent, positive onboarding experience. Reduces manual administrative burden on IT, HR, and other teams. Ensures necessary access and tools are ready on Day 1. Improves compliance and auditability of the onboarding process.

- **Cons:** High initial implementation complexity due to the need for deep cross-departmental process understanding and extensive system integrations. Maintaining the automation as processes or systems change requires ongoing effort. Requires strong collaboration and agreement between participating departments.

79. Endpoint Performance Optimization Recommendations (User-Specific)

- **Explanation:** This applies AI to diagnose common causes of endpoint (laptop/desktop) slowness based on performance data collected by endpoint agents (similar to 72, but focused on performance, not hardware failure). AI analyzes patterns in CPU usage, memory pressure, disk activity, network latency, specific application resource consumption, or known software conflicts. It correlates these patterns with known causes of poor performance (e.g., a background process consuming excessive CPU, insufficient RAM leading to swapping, disk fragmentation, browser with too many tabs, known conflicting application). Based on the diagnosis, it provides specific, easy-to-understand, actionable recommendations directly to the end-user (e.g., via a pop-up notification: "Closing unused browser tabs may improve performance," "Application 'XYZ' is using high CPU - consider restarting it") or flags the issue for automated tuning/remediation by IT (linking to self-healing concepts like 9.9 in my list or 20 in yours).

- **Implementation Strategy:** Deploy endpoint monitoring agents capable of collecting granular performance and application usage data. Feed this data into an AI engine (often within the UEM suite or AIOps platform) trained to classify common performance problems based on metric patterns. Define a library of user-facing recommendations or automated remediation actions corresponding to diagnosed issues. Deliver recommendations via agent notifications, email, chatbot, or self-service portal.
- **Pain Points Addressed:** High volume of subjective "my computer is slow" tickets hitting the Service Desk. User frustration and lost productivity due to poorly performing endpoints. Difficulty for users or L1 support to diagnose the specific cause of slowness.
- **Key AI Capability: Correlation Analysis, Classification, Root Cause Analysis (Simplified/Pattern-Based), Endpoint Telemetry Analysis.**
- **Savings/Pros:** Empowers users to self-resolve common performance issues, reducing ticket volume. Can proactively improve user experience by suggesting optimizations. Provides specific diagnoses instead of generic troubleshooting steps. May identify widespread issues caused by specific applications or updates. Reduces support costs associated with performance complaints.
- **Cons:** Users may ignore recommendations or be hesitant to act on them. Recommendations might sometimes be inaccurate or overly simplistic for complex issues. Requires effective endpoint agents and analytics capabilities. Privacy considerations around monitoring application usage. Effectiveness depends on having well-defined issue signatures and corresponding recommendations.

80. VDI Session Performance Prediction & Optimization

- **Explanation:** Virtual Desktop Infrastructure (VDI) performance is sensitive to bottlenecks anywhere along the path from the user's endpoint to the data center hosting the virtual desktop. AI specifically analyzes the complex interplay of metrics unique to VDI environments: end-user latency (Round Trip Time, often measured by the VDI protocol), bandwidth consumption, session frame rate, virtual machine resource usage on the host (CPU Ready, memory contention), storage IOPS and latency impacting the VMs, user density per host, and the health of VDI broker components. By learning normal patterns and critical thresholds, AI can predict when a user's session is likely to degrade (experience lag, stuttering, disconnects) and correlate this with likely root causes (e.g., network congestion on a specific segment, resource exhaustion on a hypervisor host, storage array overload). Based on predictions or detected issues, it can trigger proactive optimization actions like live-migrating user sessions to less loaded hosts, dynamically adjusting Quality of Service (QoS) parameters, or alerting administrators to specific infrastructure bottlenecks.

- **Implementation Strategy:** Requires specialized VDI monitoring tools (e.g., ControlUp, Goliath Technologies, eG Innovations, or native vendor tools enhanced) capable of gathering metrics from the client side, network probes, hypervisors, storage, and VDI brokers. Feed this comprehensive dataset into an AI analytics engine. Use forecasting, anomaly detection, and correlation models specific to VDI performance characteristics. Integrate with VDI management platform APIs (VMware Horizon, Citrix Virtual Apps and Desktops, AVD) to enable automated optimization actions.
- **Pain Points Addressed:** Persistent user complaints about poor VDI performance ("laggy sessions," "slow logins," disconnects). Extreme difficulty troubleshooting intermittent issues due to the complexity and multiple potential choke points in VDI environments. Inefficient use of expensive VDI infrastructure resources (either over-provisioned or hotspots causing poor experience).
- **Key AI Capability: Time-Series Forecasting, Anomaly Detection, Correlation Analysis, Optimization, VDI-Specific Metric Analysis**.
- **Savings/Pros:** Leads to a more consistent, reliable, and performant VDI user experience, improving productivity and satisfaction. Enables faster diagnosis and resolution of VDI performance problems. Allows for higher user density and more efficient utilization of VDI infrastructure resources. Reduces user complaints and associated support costs. Provides end-to-end visibility into factors affecting session performance.
- **Cons:** VDI environments are inherently complex; accurate modeling requires comprehensive data from many sources. Requires investment in specialized VDI monitoring and analytics tools, often separate from general IT monitoring. Integration with VDI management platforms for automated optimization adds complexity. Performance issues caused by the user's local network or endpoint remain challenging to fully address.

Chapter 10. Category 9: Disaster Recovery & Business Continuity (Use Cases)

81. Automated DR Plan Validation & Gap Analysis

- **Explanation:** Disaster Recovery plans, often residing in static documents (Word, PDF, Wikis), frequently lag behind the dynamic reality of the IT environment. This AI application uses Natural Language Processing (NLP) to read and interpret these human-readable DR plans, extracting key information like specified recovery sequences, application dependencies, required configurations, and RTO/RPO targets. It then programmatically compares this extracted information against the *actual* state of the environment, as discovered through CMDB data, real-time application dependency mapping tools (like 1.7/85), and infrastructure configuration scans. The AI identifies discrepancies such as servers mentioned in the plan that no longer exist, new critical application dependencies not accounted for, configuration settings that differ from recovery requirements, or recovery steps that are technically impossible with the current setup.
- **Implementation Strategy:** Requires an AI platform capable of NLP document ingestion and analysis, coupled with integrations to CMDB, discovery tools, and configuration management systems via APIs. Use NLP models (potentially requiring fine-tuning for DR plan language) to extract structured data (dependencies, configurations, sequence) from unstructured text. Employ graph analysis to compare planned dependencies vs. actual discovered dependencies. Utilize rule engines or comparison logic to flag configuration mismatches or missing components. Generate regular reports detailing inconsistencies and potential plan gaps for the BCDR team.
- **Pain Points Addressed:** DR plans becoming dangerously outdated between manual reviews. Manual validation being extremely time-consuming, infrequent, and prone to human error. Hidden dependencies or infrastructure changes silently invalidating documented recovery procedures. Lack of confidence that the plan will actually work when needed.
- **Key AI Capability: Natural Language Processing (NLP)**, **Graph Analysis**, **Data Reconciliation**, **Configuration Analysis**, **Rule Engines**.
- **Savings/Pros:** Ensures DR plans reflect the current reality much more closely, significantly reducing risk during an actual disaster. Enables continuous or frequent validation rather than slow periodic reviews. Surfaces critical gaps and inconsistencies proactively. Increases confidence in DR plan viability. Reduces manual effort required for plan maintenance and validation.
- **Cons:** NLP accuracy on complex, poorly structured, or ambiguously worded DR documents can be challenging. Success is highly dependent on the accuracy and

freshness of the CMDB and discovery data representing the "ground truth". Significant initial effort to configure NLP models and integrations. Requires clear documentation standards for DR plans to improve NLP effectiveness.

82. Predictive RTO/RPO Capability Analysis

- **Explanation:** Stated Recovery Time Objectives (RTO - how quickly services must be restored) and Recovery Point Objectives (RPO - maximum acceptable data loss) are often targets, not guarantees. This AI application provides a data-driven assessment of whether the *current* DR infrastructure and processes can actually meet these targets. It simulates DR scenarios by analyzing real-time data: current replication lag (from storage or database replication tools), recent backup completion times and data volumes, available network bandwidth between primary and recovery sites, performance benchmarks of the recovery infrastructure, and execution timings of automated recovery scripts (if used). By modeling the end-to-end recovery process using this data, AI can predict the likely RTO and RPO if a disaster occurred *now*, highlighting potential bottlenecks (e.g., insufficient network bandwidth for final data sync, slow VM boot times on recovery hardware) and quantifying the gap between predicted capability and required targets.
- **Implementation Strategy:** Requires integration with data sources from replication tools (e.g., VMware SRM, Zerto, storage array replication stats), backup systems (job completion logs, data volumes), network monitoring tools (bandwidth utilization/latency on replication links), performance monitoring in the DR site, and potentially logs from recovery automation tools. Utilize simulation modeling and time-series forecasting (e.g., to predict data sync times based on current lag and bandwidth). Generate regular reports showing predicted RTO/RPO vs. target for critical applications, along with identified bottleneck contributors.
- **Pain Points Addressed:** Uncertainty about whether defined RTO/RPO targets are realistically achievable with the current setup. RTO/RPO commitments based on assumptions or outdated test results rather than current operational data. Difficulty identifying specific bottlenecks hindering faster recovery or minimizing data loss. Lack of quantitative justification for DR infrastructure investments or process improvements.
- **Key AI Capability: Simulation, Time-Series Forecasting, Bottleneck Analysis, Correlation Analysis.**
- **Savings/Pros:** Provides a realistic, data-driven assessment of DR readiness against business requirements. Pinpoints specific technological or process bottlenecks that need addressing to meet targets. Helps prioritize DR investments effectively. Provides quantitative evidence for discussions with business stakeholders about achievable recovery levels. Reduces the risk of failing to meet objectives during a real event.
- **Cons:** Simulation accuracy depends heavily on the quality and timeliness of input data from various systems. Accurately modeling complex, multi-stage recovery processes can be difficult. Unexpected failures or factors during a real event might not be captured in

the simulation. Requires investment in tools capable of sophisticated simulation and data integration.

83.Optimal DR Site/Resource Selection & Cost Modeling

- **Explanation:** Choosing the right Disaster Recovery strategy involves complex trade-offs between cost, performance (RTO/RPO), compliance, and management overhead. AI assists in this strategic decision-making by modeling and comparing different DR options. These options could include building/maintaining a secondary data center, utilizing specific cloud provider regions (IaaS/PaaS), leveraging Disaster Recovery as a Service (DRaaS) offerings, or employing hybrid approaches. The AI considers the specific RTO/RPO and compliance requirements (e.g., data residency) for different applications, ingests current pricing information for compute, storage, networking, data egress, and specialized DR services from relevant providers, and then uses optimization algorithms to recommend the most cost-effective solution mix that meets all constraints.
- **Implementation Strategy:** Define clear RTO/RPO tiers and compliance requirements per application or group. Gather up-to-date pricing data from potential DR sites/providers (secondary DC costs, cloud price lists, DRaaS quotes). Develop or utilize cost modeling and optimization tools that can simulate the costs of replicating, maintaining infrastructure/services, and recovering various workloads under each scenario. Present a comparative analysis of options ranked by cost-effectiveness while meeting requirements.
- **Pain Points Addressed:** Difficulty objectively comparing the complex cost structures and capabilities of diverse DR solutions. Risk of selecting an overly expensive DR strategy or one that fails to meet recovery needs. Controlling the often significant ongoing costs associated with DR readiness. Ensuring compliance requirements are met by the chosen solution.
- **Key AI Capability: Optimization, Cost Modeling, Simulation, Constraint Programming**.
- **Savings/Pros:** Enables selection of the most cost-efficient DR strategy that demonstrably meets business requirements. Potential for significant savings on DR infrastructure and service costs. Provides a data-driven basis for strategic DR architecture decisions. Ensures compliance and RTO/RPO needs are factored into the financial analysis. Facilitates comparison of TCO across different DR models.
- **Cons:** Cloud and DRaaS pricing models are complex and change frequently, requiring continuous updates to the cost models. Accurately defining all requirements and constraints upfront is critical. Models may not capture all hidden costs or operational nuances. Requires expertise in both DR technologies and financial modeling.

84.Automated DR Test Orchestration & Validation

- **Explanation:** Traditional DR testing is often a manual, disruptive, and infrequent exercise. This use case applies automation, potentially guided by AI, to execute DR tests more efficiently and reliably. Based on the documented (or dynamically generated - see

85) DR plan, automation tools orchestrate the sequence of actions: failing over replication, bringing up virtual machines and applications in the recovery site, configuring network settings, and crucially, running predefined validation scripts or tests to confirm that applications are functioning correctly and data integrity is maintained (e.g., checking database connectivity, performing synthetic transactions, verifying key services). AI could potentially optimize the test sequence for speed or resource usage, or analyze test results to automatically determine pass/fail status. The entire process, including validation results, is automatically logged for audit purposes.

- **Implementation Strategy:** Requires codifying DR test procedures into automated workflows or runbooks using tools like VMware SRM, Azure Site Recovery orchestration plans, Ansible, Terraform, or specialized Runbook Automation platforms. Develop robust validation scripts for critical applications. Integrate automation tools with hypervisors, cloud APIs, network devices, and potentially monitoring tools in the recovery site. AI components could select optimal test sequences or apply machine learning to analyze validation results for anomalies. Schedule and execute automated tests regularly.

- **Pain Points Addressed:** Manual DR testing is extremely time-consuming, resource-intensive, and prone to human error. Testing often disrupts production or requires significant downtime windows. Infrequent testing leads to lack of confidence and outdated procedures. Documenting test results manually is laborious and inconsistent.

- **Key AI Capability: Workflow Automation, Scripting, Automated Testing, Orchestration,** (Optional AI: **Scheduling Optimization, Result Analysis**).

- **Savings/Pros:** Drastically reduces the manual effort and time required for DR testing (Est: >70% effort reduction achievable). Enables more frequent, potentially non-disruptive ("bubble network") testing, increasing confidence and readiness. Ensures consistent and repeatable test execution. Provides automated documentation for audit compliance. Faster identification of issues in the recovery process.

- **Cons:** Significant initial investment required to develop and maintain the automation scripts and validation checks for each application/service. Automation needs to be rigorously tested itself to avoid causing issues during a test or actual event. Requires skilled personnel to build and manage the automation framework.

85. Dynamic Application Recovery Sequence Generation

- **Explanation:** Static DR plans often define a fixed recovery sequence for applications, which can become incorrect as application architectures evolve and dependencies change. This AI capability leverages real-time or frequently updated application dependency mapping data (from discovery tools, CMDB, APM, or service mesh telemetry) to dynamically generate the *correct* recovery sequence at the time of a DR event or test. Using graph traversal algorithms (like topological sort), it ensures that foundational services (e.g., Active Directory, DNS, core databases) are recovered before the applications that depend on them, preventing failures caused by incorrect startup order. This sequence can then be fed into automated DR orchestration tools (like 84).

- **Implementation Strategy:** Requires access to an accurate, up-to-date application dependency map (this is often the biggest prerequisite challenge, potentially generated by tools mentioned in 1.7 or similar). Implement graph algorithms (e.g., topological sort) that consume the dependency map and output a valid recovery sequence (potentially in multiple parallel stages where dependencies allow). Integrate the output sequence generator with the DR automation/orchestration platform.
- **Pain Points Addressed:** Manually defined recovery sequences in DR plans are often wrong or incomplete due to complex and changing application dependencies. Recovering applications in the wrong order leads to failures, delays, and manual troubleshooting during a critical DR event. Keeping dependency documentation up-to-date manually is extremely difficult.
- **Key AI Capability: Dependency Graph Analysis, Topological Sort, Real-time Data Integration.**
- **Savings/Pros:** Ensures applications are recovered in the correct order based on actual dependencies, significantly increasing the reliability and speed of the recovery process. Reduces errors and manual intervention caused by dependency issues during DR. Adapts automatically to changes in the application landscape if the dependency map is kept current. Provides a more robust foundation for DR automation.
- **Cons:** Critically dependent on the existence and accuracy of the application dependency map. If the map is inaccurate, the generated sequence will be wrong. Requires tools or processes to maintain the dependency map effectively. Integration with DR orchestration tools is necessary to execute the dynamic sequence.

86. Real-time Risk Assessment During DR Events/Tests

- **Explanation:** During the high-stress execution phase of a DR test or an actual disaster failover, it's difficult for the command team to maintain situational awareness and quickly identify emerging problems. AI assists by continuously monitoring the progress of the recovery against the planned timeline and expected outcomes. It ingests real-time data from the DR orchestration tool's logs, monitoring systems in the recovery environment (VM status, performance metrics, network connectivity), and replication/backup tools (data sync status). AI algorithms (anomaly detection, correlation, rule engines) compare the actual progress to the plan, flag significant delays, detect unexpected errors (e.g., VMs failing to boot, validation checks failing, higher-than-expected error rates), and highlight resource constraints or bottlenecks as they emerge. This information is presented on a real-time dashboard, providing an objective risk assessment and drawing attention to critical deviations requiring immediate management intervention.
- **Implementation Strategy:** Requires integrating logs and metrics from DR automation tools, monitoring systems (infrastructure & application in the recovery site), and potentially replication/backup tools into a centralized AIOps or command center platform during the event. Implement AI models to detect anomalies relative to the plan or expected behavior (e.g., a step taking much longer than planned, error rates spiking).

Configure rules to identify critical failure conditions. Visualize key progress indicators, deviations, and AI-detected risks on a dashboard for the DR command team.

- **Pain Points Addressed:** Lack of clear, real-time visibility into the overall status and progress during chaotic DR events or complex tests. Unexpected problems going unnoticed until they cause major delays or failures. Difficulty prioritizing issues requiring immediate attention. Subjective assessment of progress and risk.
- **Key AI Capability: Correlation Analysis, Anomaly Detection, Real-time Analytics, Rule Engines, Data Visualization**.
- **Savings/Pros:** Greatly improves situational awareness for the DR command team. Enables faster identification and prioritization of emerging issues hindering the recovery process. Facilitates quicker decision-making to address roadblocks. Provides an objective measure of progress against the plan and expected RTO. Reduces the likelihood of test failures or prolonged outages due to undetected problems.
- **Cons:** Requires significant real-time data integration effort, specifically tailored for the duration of the DR event/test. Setting up meaningful dashboards and alerts requires careful planning. AI interpretation of "risk" needs to be well-calibrated to avoid excessive noise or missed critical events.

87. Post-DR Test Performance & Bottleneck Analysis

- **Explanation:** After completing a DR test, simply knowing whether applications recovered is often insufficient; understanding *how well* they performed in the recovery environment is crucial for true readiness. This AI application focuses on analyzing the detailed performance metrics and logs collected *during* the DR test execution. It correlates data from applications, servers, storage, and networking within the recovery site to identify any performance bottlenecks that occurred. Examples include discovering that storage IOPS were insufficient for database workloads under load, identifying network congestion between recovered application tiers, or pinpointing specific VMs that were CPU-starved. This analysis provides concrete insights for optimizing the DR environment's resource provisioning and configuration.
- **Implementation Strategy:** Requires comprehensive performance data collection (CPU, memory, network, disk I/O, application response times) from relevant systems in the recovery environment throughout the duration of the DR test. After the test, feed this data into an analytics platform (AIOps, performance management tools). Use AI techniques like correlation analysis, resource saturation analysis, and bottleneck detection algorithms to pinpoint performance constraints and their likely causes. Generate post-test reports detailing findings and recommendations for optimizing the DR site resources.
- **Pain Points Addressed:** Applications recover during a DR test but perform poorly, potentially missing RTO if users can't actually use them effectively. Difficulty pinpointing the root cause of poor performance in the recovery environment after the test is over. DR environments often undersized due to cost pressures, leading to unexpected

bottlenecks under load. Uncertainty about whether the DR site can handle production load.

- **Key AI Capability: Correlation Analysis, Performance Analysis, Bottleneck Analysis, Resource Usage Modeling**.
- **Savings/Pros:** Provides actionable insights to optimize the performance of the DR environment, ensuring applications are usable after recovery. Helps accurately size DR resources, balancing cost and performance. Reduces the risk of failing to meet true business recovery needs due to performance issues. Justifies necessary investments in the DR site infrastructure based on test data.
- **Cons:** Requires implementing robust performance data collection mechanisms specifically for the DR test period. Analysis is performed post-test, not in real-time. Interpreting complex performance interactions may still require expert analysis. Can be challenging if applications behave very differently under test conditions vs. real load.

88. Backup Job Success/Failure Prediction

- **Explanation:** Backup failures can jeopardize RPO and leave data unprotected. This AI capability aims to predict the likelihood of specific backup jobs failing *before* they run. It analyzes historical patterns from backup system logs (past successes/failures, error messages, durations), correlates them with infrastructure metrics around the typical backup window (e.g., network load, storage performance, server resource usage), and considers job characteristics (data volume, source type). By identifying recurring failure patterns or precursor conditions (e.g., jobs targeting a specific server often fail when its CPU is high, network latency spikes usually cause failures for remote backups), the AI can flag upcoming jobs with a high probability of failure, allowing backup administrators to proactively investigate and remediate the underlying cause.
- **Implementation Strategy:** Collect and centralize historical backup job logs/status and relevant infrastructure performance metrics from the time windows when backups typically run. Train AI classification models (e.g., logistic regression, decision trees, neural networks) to predict the outcome (success/failure) of future jobs based on historical patterns and current/predicted conditions. Integrate predictions into backup monitoring dashboards or generate alerts for jobs deemed high-risk.
- **Pain Points Addressed:** Unexpected backup failures discovered only after they occur, leading to potential RPO violations and data exposure. Repetitive failures caused by underlying issues that aren't proactively addressed. Wasted resources attempting jobs that are likely to fail. Reactive troubleshooting of backup failures.
- **Key AI Capability: Classification, Time-Series Forecasting** (of infrastructure load), **Anomaly Detection** (in job behavior), **Log Analysis**.
- **Savings/Pros:** Allows proactive intervention to prevent backup failures (Est: predict >80% of recurring failures), significantly improving backup success rates. Leads to more reliable RPO adherence and reduced risk of data loss. Saves time spent reactively troubleshooting failed jobs. Optimizes resource usage by avoiding predictably failing jobs (or fixing the cause first).

- **Cons:** Requires access to detailed historical backup job data and correlated infrastructure metrics. Failure causes can be diverse and complex, making prediction challenging for non-recurring issues. Models need retraining as the environment changes. Requires integration with backup software monitoring.

89. Silent Data Corruption Detection in Backups/Replicas

- **Explanation:** A particularly insidious risk is "silent" data corruption, where data is altered subtly due to hardware faults, software bugs, or bit rot, but the backup or replication process itself completes without error. This AI application provides enhanced methods to detect such corruption beyond simple job success checks. Techniques include: automating periodic, end-to-end checksum comparisons between source data and backup/replica copies; using statistical analysis or anomaly detection on data patterns within backup sets (e.g., unusual changes in compressibility, abnormal data block distributions) that might indicate corruption; and orchestrating more intelligent, automated test restores that perform deep validation checks (e.g., application-level consistency checks, database integrity checks) on a sampled basis.
- **Implementation Strategy:** Implement robust checksumming at various layers if possible. Feed backup metadata or data samples into AI anomaly detection models trained on normal data characteristics. Develop automated test restore workflows (using tools like in 84) that include application-specific validation scripts. Schedule these enhanced validation checks periodically based on data criticality and risk tolerance.
- **Pain Points Addressed:** The critical risk of successfully recovering data that is found to be corrupted and unusable only after recovery. Basic backup success/failure reporting provides a false sense of security. Difficulty detecting gradual or subtle data degradation over time. Compliance requirements for data integrity validation.
- **Key AI Capability: Hashing/Checksumming Validation, Anomaly Detection, Statistical Analysis, Automated Testing & Validation.**
- **Savings/Pros:** Significantly increases confidence in the integrity and recoverability of backup and replicated data. Enables early detection of silent corruption before it spreads or renders backups useless. Helps meet compliance requirements for data integrity. Reduces the risk of catastrophic data loss upon recovery.
- **Cons:** Full data checksumming or comparison can be extremely computationally intensive and time-consuming, often impractical for large datasets. Sampling methods provide probabilistic, not guaranteed, detection. Defining "normal" data patterns for anomaly detection can be complex. Requires sophisticated automation for test restores with deep validation.

90. Automated Replication Health Monitoring & Issue Prediction

- **Explanation:** Continuous data replication is fundamental to achieving low RPO targets. This AI capability focuses on monitoring the health and performance of data replication processes (whether storage array-based, hypervisor-based, or database-native replication). It analyzes key replication metrics such as replication lag (the time delay between data changing on the source and being written to the replica), throughput (data transfer rate), error rates, buffer usage, and the performance of the network path between sites. By establishing baselines for these metrics, AI can detect anomalies (e.g., lag suddenly increasing, throughput dropping) and use forecasting techniques to predict when replication lag might exceed the defined RPO threshold or when a potential replication failure is imminent. This provides early warning to storage, database, or network administrators to investigate and resolve issues proactively.

- **Implementation Strategy:** Requires collecting detailed performance metrics specifically from the replication tools or platforms being used (often via APIs or dedicated monitoring interfaces). Feed this time-series data into AI models (anomaly detection, time-series forecasting) within an AIOps or specialized monitoring platform. Configure alerting based on detected anomalies or predictions of exceeding RPO thresholds. Correlate replication metrics with network performance data if possible.

- **Pain Points Addressed:** Replication lag growing excessive without being noticed until an audit or attempted failover, jeopardizing RPO. Unexpected replication link saturation or failures halting data protection. Difficulty troubleshooting intermittent replication performance issues. Lack of proactive alerting on degrading replication health.

- **Key AI Capability: Anomaly Detection, Time-Series Forecasting, Correlation Analysis**.

- **Savings/Pros:** Enables proactive identification and resolution of replication problems before they impact RPO commitments. Provides better assurance of meeting data protection objectives. Reduces the risk of significant data loss during a disaster. Faster detection and diagnosis of replication issues. Optimizes replication performance and network usage.

- **Cons:** Requires specific integration to gather metrics from diverse replication technologies (storage vendors, database vendors, hypervisor tools). Predictive accuracy depends on the stability and predictability of workload and network conditions. May require tuning to avoid alerts for transient, non-critical fluctuations.

Chapter 11. Category 10: Compliance & Governance (Use Cases)

91. Automated Compliance Evidence Collection & Aggregation

- **Explanation:** Streamlines audit preparation by automating the gathering of evidence required by compliance frameworks (PCI-DSS, HIPAA, SOX, ISO 27001, etc.). This replaces manual efforts by mapping control requirements to specific digital evidence (configuration files, logs, reports). Automation tools (RPA bots, scripts, integrations) connect to IT systems (servers, databases, firewalls, cloud consoles, vulnerability scanners, log management systems) via APIs or command lines to extract necessary data. Collected evidence is then aggregated, timestamped, tagged, and stored in a central GRC platform for auditor review.
- **Implementation Strategy:** Requires detailed mapping of compliance controls to evidence sources. Utilize automation platforms (RPA, scripting, API integration within GRC tools) with secure credentials to access target systems. Define collection schedules (quarterly, monthly, continuous). Store evidence in a structured repository within a GRC tool, ensuring integrity and linkage to control requirements. NLP can be used to parse control requirements for easier evidence source identification.
- **Pain Points Addressed:** Reduces hundreds/thousands of manual hours spent on audit preparation. Minimizes human error in evidence collection. Ensures consistent evidence gathering across systems and time. Enables on-demand or continuous compliance demonstration. Alleviates last-minute audit stress and disruption.
- **Key AI Capability:** Workflow Automation, Robotic Process Automation (RPA), API Integration, Data Aggregation, Optional NLP (parsing control requirements).
- **Savings/Pros:** Drastic reduction (60-80%) in manual effort for evidence gathering. Improved accuracy and consistency of evidence. Enables "continuous compliance readiness." Frees up IT staff from tedious tasks. Provides a clear, automated audit trail. Potentially reduces audit duration and cost.
- **Cons:** Significant initial setup to map controls to evidence sources and configure automation. Requires robust security for automation tool credentials. Maintenance needed for system and compliance changes. May not automate all evidence types (e.g., policy attestations). Relies on API availability and stability.

92. Continuous Configuration Compliance Monitoring & Alerting

- **Explanation:** Ensures IT systems consistently adhere to security configuration baselines (CIS Benchmarks, DISA STIGs) or regulatory requirements. Continuously monitors the configuration state of servers, network devices, databases, and cloud services against predefined "desired state" policies. AI-powered policy engines or specialized tools (CSPM for cloud) automatically scan configurations via agents or APIs, compare them to baseline templates (often as code), and detect unauthorized changes ("configuration drift"). Non-compliant settings trigger automatic alerts to relevant teams via ITSM or notifications, often including deviation details and potentially initiating automated remediation.

- **Implementation Strategy:** Define clear, machine-readable security configuration baselines and policies (YAML, JSON, specialized languages). Deploy configuration scanning tools, endpoint management agents with compliance modules, or CSPM tools. Utilize AI/policy engines to compare actual vs. desired state. Configure alerting rules and thresholds. Integrate alerts with ITSM for ticketing and potentially with automation tools (Ansible, Chef, Puppet) for automated fixes.
- **Pain Points Addressed:** Prevents unnoticed configuration drift between manual audits, leading to compliance failures and vulnerabilities. Addresses slow, infrequent, and sampling-based manual auditing. Enforces consistent configurations across complex environments. Mitigates security risks from systems reverting to insecure defaults or misconfigurations.
- **Key AI Capability:** Policy Engines, Configuration Analysis, Anomaly Detection (detecting drift), Desired State Configuration Management (DSCM) principles.
- **Savings/Pros:** Real-time detection and alerting on compliance violations and misconfigurations, enabling rapid remediation. Significantly reduces audit findings related to configuration issues. Improves overall security posture through consistent hardening. Provides continuous visibility into compliance status. Facilitates automated remediation of common drifts.
- **Cons:** Requires significant effort to define and maintain accurate baselines and policies across diverse technologies. Can generate alert noise if policies are too strict or poorly defined. Automated remediation carries risks if not thoroughly tested. Requires investment in appropriate scanning/monitoring tools.

93. Anomalous Data Access Pattern Detection for Privacy Compliance

- **Explanation:** Monitors access to sensitive personal data (PII, PHI) to detect potentially inappropriate or malicious activity, crucial for regulations like GDPR, CCPA, and HIPAA. Identifies systems storing sensitive data and ingests their access audit logs. AI, using UEBA techniques, establishes baseline patterns of normal access for users and roles (volume, time, location, query types). Detects statistically significant anomalies like large downloads, access to unrelated data, unusual hours, or failed attempts followed by success, indicating potential breaches or insider threats.
- **Implementation Strategy:** Requires accurate identification and classification of sensitive data stores (using data discovery tools). Ensure comprehensive audit logging on these systems and central ingestion into a SIEM or security analytics platform with UEBA. Configure UEBA models focused on sensitive data access, defining peer groups and

acceptable behavior. Tune anomaly detection rules to minimize false positives. Route high-priority alerts to SOC and/or Privacy/Compliance teams.

- **Pain Points Addressed:** Addresses the extreme difficulty of manually monitoring vast access logs for sensitive data. Overcomes limitations of simple rule-based alerts that miss subtle misuse. Enables proactive discovery of privacy breaches, avoiding reactive responses and missed reporting deadlines. Provides evidence of adequate monitoring controls for auditors.
- **Key AI Capability:** Anomaly Detection, User and Entity Behavior Analytics (UEBA), Behavioral Profiling, Peer Group Analysis, Data Classification awareness.
- **Savings/Pros:** Proactive detection of potential data breaches or insider misuse, allowing for faster containment. Helps meet stringent regulatory requirements for monitoring personal data access. Reduces the risk of fines and reputational damage from privacy violations. Provides forensic evidence for investigations. Focuses security team attention on genuine risks.
- **Cons:** Effectiveness heavily depends on accurate data classification and the quality/completeness of access audit logs. UEBA systems can generate false positives, requiring tuning and investigation. Defining "normal" access can be complex for roles with broad access needs. Requires careful consideration of privacy concerns around user activity monitoring.

94. AI-Assisted Audit Log Review for Control Failures

- **Explanation:** Enhances traditional audit log review by automating the pre-processing of logs. Instead of manual sampling or keyword searches, AI uses anomaly detection to identify unusual entries, pattern recognition to spot known indicators of control bypasses, and clustering to group similar suspicious events. Auditors receive a prioritized list of potentially significant events, allowing them to focus on high-risk areas identified by the AI.
- **Implementation Strategy:** Requires centralizing diverse audit logs (OS, application, database, network, cloud) into a SIEM or log analytics platform with AI capabilities. Train or utilize AI models (anomaly detection, pattern matching, clustering) on historical log data. Configure the system to generate prioritized outputs (alerts, dashboards, reports) designed for auditors, highlighting suspicious findings with context.
- **Pain Points Addressed:** Overcomes the time-consuming, tedious, and often ineffective nature of manual audit log review. Addresses the risk of missing critical events due to reliance on sampling. Solves the "needle in a haystack" problem of massive log volumes. Improves the ability to demonstrate effective log review practices.
- **Key AI Capability:** Anomaly Detection, Pattern Recognition, Clustering, Log Parsing/Normalization, Risk Scoring.
- **Savings/Pros:** Significantly improves the efficiency and effectiveness of audit log review. Increases the likelihood of detecting actual control weaknesses, errors, or malicious activity. Provides a more systematic and defensible approach than manual sampling. Can

accelerate audit processes. Helps meet log review requirements for compliance frameworks.
  - **Cons:** AI analysis might miss novel or highly sophisticated attacks not matching trained patterns. Findings still require interpretation and validation by experienced auditors. Requires investment in capable log analytics platforms and AI engines. Tuning models to minimize false positives is crucial.

95. Regulatory Change Impact Assessment on IT Policies/Controls

- **Explanation:** Automates the initial assessment of how new or updated regulations impact IT policies, standards, and controls. Uses NLP to compare new regulatory texts (e.g., GDPR ruling, updated PCI-DSS) against the organization's existing documentation. The AI identifies overlapping concepts, changed requirements, new obligations, and potential conflicts, highlighting specific internal policies or controls needing review and updates.
- **Implementation Strategy:** Requires digitizing and indexing both external regulatory documents and internal IT policy/control libraries in a format suitable for NLP analysis. Utilize AI platforms or specialized GRC tools with NLP capabilities (document comparison, semantic analysis, topic modeling, entity recognition) tuned for legal/regulatory language. Configure the AI to map regulatory clauses to internal control objectives or policy sections. Present identified potential impacts and required updates to compliance and policy teams.
- **Pain Points Addressed:** Reduces the extremely time-consuming and expert-driven manual process of analyzing new regulations. Minimizes the high risk of overlooking critical changes or misinterpreting requirements, leading to non-compliance. Prevents delays in updating internal policies after new regulations. Improves tracking of the lineage between external requirements and internal controls.
- **Key AI Capability:** Natural Language Processing (NLP) (Document Comparison, Semantic Analysis, Topic Modeling, Entity Recognition).
- **Savings/Pros:** Significantly accelerates the identification of IT policies and controls impacted by regulatory changes. Reduces the risk of non-compliance from missed updates. Frees up compliance and legal experts for higher-level interpretation and strategy. Ensures a more systematic and thorough review of regulatory impacts. Helps maintain an up-to-date control framework.
- **Cons:** NLP accuracy depends heavily on the complexity, structure, and clarity of both regulatory texts and internal documents. AI provides potential impact areas; human expertise is still needed for final interpretation and rewriting. Requires maintaining comprehensive, machine-readable libraries of regulations and internal policies. May require specialized NLP tools or significant tuning.

96.Automated Generation of Compliance Attestation Reports

- **Explanation:** Automates the creation of standardized attestation reports (e.g., PCI AoC, SOC 2, internal dashboards) by pulling data directly from underlying systems. This includes control status from monitoring tools, links to automatically collected evidence, vulnerability scan summaries, patch compliance metrics, and potentially DR test results. The data is used to automatically populate predefined report templates, minimizing manual intervention.
- **Implementation Strategy:** Requires integration between a reporting tool or GRC platform and systems holding compliance data and evidence (monitoring tools, evidence repositories, vulnerability scanners, patch management, etc.) via APIs. Define standardized report templates. Use workflow automation or reporting engines to query data sources and populate templates on a schedule or on demand. Ensure mechanisms for human review and approval, especially for external reports.
- **Pain Points Addressed:** Eliminates the extremely time-consuming, repetitive, and error-prone manual compilation of compliance reports. Addresses the issue of reports becoming outdated quickly. Ensures consistency across different reports and reporting periods. Reduces effort spent formatting and validating data.
- **Key AI Capability:** Report Generation Automation, Workflow Automation, Data Aggregation, API Integration.
- **Savings/Pros:** Dramatically reduces manual effort and time for generating routine compliance reports (50%+ reduction). Ensures reports are based on the latest data, improving accuracy and timeliness. Increases consistency in report format and content. Enables faster availability of reports for review. Frees up compliance teams for higher-value activities.
- **Cons:** The quality and accuracy of automated reports depend entirely on the underlying data sources. Requires well-defined and standardized report templates. Significant initial effort to set up integrations and templates. Human review and sign-off remain essential for formal attestations.

97.AI-Driven IT Risk Assessment Based on Control Effectiveness

- **Explanation:** Creates a more objective, data-driven, and dynamic view of IT risk, moving beyond subjective scoring and infrequent assessments. Integrates data from multiple sources reflecting actual control performance and threat landscape: automated control test results, vulnerability scanning data, incident management records, threat intelligence feeds, and asset criticality information. AI risk scoring models correlate these factors to calculate quantitative risk scores for different IT assets, systems, or processes.
- **Implementation Strategy:** Requires integrating data feeds from GRC platforms, vulnerability management tools, ITSM, threat intelligence platforms, and the CMDB into a central risk analytics engine. Develop or utilize AI risk scoring models (Bayesian networks, machine learning classifiers) that quantify risk based on combined inputs.

Visualize risk scores on dynamic dashboards with drill-down capabilities. Regularly refresh data and recalculate scores.

- **Pain Points Addressed:** Addresses the subjectivity, inconsistency, and rapid obsolescence of traditional IT risk assessments. Overcomes the difficulty of prioritizing mitigation efforts based on objective data. Provides better visibility into the actual effectiveness of controls. Enables continuous risk monitoring instead of periodic exercises.
- **Key AI Capability:** Risk Scoring Models, Machine Learning (Classification/Regression), Data Correlation, Threat Intelligence Integration, Control Effectiveness Measurement.
- **Savings/Pros:** Provides a more objective, data-driven, and dynamic view of IT risk. Enables better prioritization of security investments and risk mitigation. Helps demonstrate the effectiveness of security controls. Facilitates continuous risk monitoring. Improves communication about risk using quantitative data.
- **Cons:** High implementation complexity due to the need to integrate and correlate data from diverse systems. Developing accurate and meaningful risk scoring models requires significant expertise and validation. Transparency of complex AI models can be a challenge. Requires high-quality input data from all integrated sources.

98. Data Residency Policy Validation & Enforcement Monitoring

- **Explanation:** Helps organizations monitor and enforce data residency policies mandated by regulations like GDPR. Leverages data discovery and classification tools (potentially using AI/ML) to identify repositories containing sensitive data subject to residency rules. Monitors cloud service configurations and analyzes network traffic to track where this data resides and if it's being moved across geographical boundaries. AI-driven policy engines compare data locations and movements against defined policies, generating alerts for potential violations.
- **Implementation Strategy:** Deploy robust data discovery and classification tools. Integrate with cloud configuration monitoring (CSPM) tools and potentially network flow analysis tools. Define data residency policies clearly within a policy engine (GRC or security platforms). Configure the AI policy engine to continuously compare discovered data locations and detected cross-border flows against these policies. Route alerts to appropriate teams.
- **Pain Points Addressed:** Addresses the extreme difficulty of manually tracking sensitive data residency in complex hybrid environments. Prevents accidental movement or replication of data to non-compliant locations. Improves the ability to prove compliance with data residency regulations. Mitigates the risk of significant fines for violating data sovereignty laws.
- **Key AI Capability:** Data Discovery, Data Classification, Policy Engines, Network Flow Analysis, Cloud Configuration Monitoring.
- **Savings/Pros:** Provides automated monitoring and alerting for potential data residency violations, significantly reducing compliance risk. Helps maintain an accurate inventory of sensitive data locations. Provides crucial evidence for demonstrating compliance.

Enables faster detection and correction of policy violations. Reduces the risk of substantial regulatory fines.

- **Cons:** Accurate and comprehensive data discovery and classification at scale remains a major technical challenge. Visibility into encrypted network traffic is limited. Cloud provider services and configurations are complex and evolving. False positives are possible.

99. Intelligent Access Recertification Candidate Suggestion

- **Explanation:** Makes user access reviews more focused and effective by analyzing user access entitlements against contextual factors. This includes actual usage logs, entitlements of peers, recent role changes, and the inherent risk level of the entitlement. AI flags specific access rights within the review list that are high-risk and warrant closer scrutiny by the reviewing manager, guiding them away from blanket approvals.
- **Implementation Strategy:** Integrate the access certification tool (IGA platforms) with sources of contextual data: Identity Management system, application usage logs, HR system, and potentially a risk classification for entitlements. Utilize AI models (anomaly detection, peer group analysis, rule engines) to score the risk level of each entitlement. Clearly highlight or prioritize high-risk items within the manager's review interface.
- **Pain Points Addressed:** Addresses the issue of access review campaigns becoming a "rubber-stamping" exercise. Overcomes managers being overwhelmed by the number of entitlements to review. Helps combat the gradual accumulation of excessive user permissions ("privilege creep"). Improves the effectiveness of access review controls.
- **Key AI Capability:** Anomaly Detection, Peer Group Analysis, Usage Pattern Analysis, Risk Scoring, Data Correlation.
- **Savings/Pros:** Significantly improves the effectiveness of user access reviews by focusing attention on high-risk entitlements. Helps combat privilege creep and enforce least privilege. Reduces the organizational attack surface. Provides a more defensible and intelligent access certification process. Potentially reduces manager time spent on low-risk reviews.
- **Cons:** Requires reliable access to entitlement usage logs, which may not be available for all systems. Defining appropriate peer groups and "normal" access patterns can be complex. Managers may still ignore suggestions if not properly trained. Requires a capable IGA platform with AI features or integration with external AI tools.

100. Automated Patch Compliance Reporting & Exception Tracking

- **Explanation:** Streamlines the tracking and reporting of patch compliance by automatically correlating data from vulnerability scanners and patch deployment tools. Based on defined policies, it calculates compliance percentages. It also manages the workflow for documented exceptions, flagging expiring exceptions and routing requests for new exceptions through a formal approval process, ensuring clear documentation of accepted risks.

- **Implementation Strategy:** Requires integrating data feeds from vulnerability management tools, patch management systems, and the ITSM/GRC platform. Use automation scripts or platform integrations to correlate vulnerability/missing patch data with deployment status. Implement reporting dashboards showing compliance rates. Configure workflows within ITSM/GRC to handle patch exceptions.
- **Pain Points Addressed:** Eliminates the manual, time-consuming, and error-prone process of correlating vulnerability scan results with patch deployment status. Addresses the difficulty of tracking patch exception status and approval history. Simplifies the generation of accurate compliance reports. Provides real-time visibility into overall patch posture.
- **Key AI Capability:** Data Correlation, Reporting Automation, Workflow Management, Policy Enforcement Checking. (Note: AI aspect is lighter, mostly correlation and automation, but could involve AI for predicting patch success or risk scoring exceptions).
- **Savings/Pros:** Provides near real-time, accurate visibility into patch compliance status (70%+ effort reduction in reporting). Simplifies and accelerates compliance reporting for audits. Ensures a standardized and auditable process for managing patch exceptions. Helps prioritize remediation efforts on non-compliant systems. Improves overall security posture.
- **Cons:** Relies heavily on the accuracy and timeliness of data from both vulnerability scanners and patch deployment tools. Discrepancies between tools require investigation. Defining and managing the exception workflow process requires careful setup. Does not fundamentally solve the problem of applying patches faster, but improves visibility and tracking.

Chapter 12. Category 11: IT Strategy & Financial Planning (Use Cases)

101. Predictive IT Budget Forecasting (OpEx/CapEx Breakdown)

- **Explanation:** Enhances traditional IT budgeting by using AI to ingest a wider range of data inputs beyond historical trends. This includes historical spending (OpEx/CapEx breakdown), project portfolio management (PPM) data, infrastructure asset data (lifecycle, refresh dates), detailed cloud usage forecasts (from FinOps tools), and even relevant business forecasts (headcount growth, new product launches). Using time-series forecasting and regression models, AI can generate more accurate, granular budget predictions broken down by cost center, service, or project, anticipating future needs more reliably than simple extrapolation.
- **Implementation Strategy:** Requires aggregating and cleansing data from various sources: ERP/Financial systems (historical spend), PPM tools, Asset Management databases (CMDB), Cloud billing portals/FinOps tools, and potentially business planning systems. Apply appropriate AI models (time-series like ARIMA, Prophet, or regression models incorporating multiple variables). Segment the data for granular forecasts (by cost center, service). Visualize forecasts and allow for scenario planning (e.g., impact of delaying a hardware refresh). Regularly retrain models with new data.
- **Pain Points Addressed:** Inaccurate budgets leading to overspending or underfunding. Difficulty anticipating future IT needs and costs. Reactive budgeting instead of proactive planning. Limited visibility into the drivers of IT spending. Challenges in justifying budget requests to business stakeholders.
- **Key AI Capability:** Time Series Forecasting, Regression Analysis, Data Integration, Scenario Planning.
- **Savings/Pros:** More accurate budget forecasts reduce financial waste and improve resource allocation. Enables proactive planning and investment decisions. Provides data-driven justification for budget requests. Improves alignment between IT spending and business goals. Reduces the risk of budget surprises and overruns.
- **Cons:** Requires significant effort to integrate and cleanse data from disparate systems. Accuracy of forecasts depends on the quality and completeness of input data. AI models can be complex and require specialized expertise to build and maintain. External factors (economic changes, unexpected business shifts) can still impact actual spending.

102. Automated IT Asset Lifecycle Management & Optimization

- **Explanation:** Manually tracking the lifecycle of IT assets (hardware, software licenses, cloud instances) is complex and often leads to inefficiencies like paying for unused licenses or facing unexpected hardware failures. AI can automate and optimize this process. It ingests data from asset management systems, procurement records, usage monitoring tools, and vendor contracts. AI models can predict when hardware is likely to fail (predictive maintenance), identify underutilized software licenses, and optimize cloud resource allocation based on actual usage patterns. This helps organizations proactively plan for replacements, reclaim unused resources, and negotiate better vendor deals.

- **Implementation Strategy:** Integrate data from asset management systems (CMDB), procurement systems, monitoring tools (for usage), and contract management systems. Utilize AI models for time-series forecasting (predicting failures), clustering (identifying similar asset usage patterns), and optimization algorithms (for cloud resource allocation). Implement automated alerts for upcoming renewals, end-of-life assets, or potential cost savings from resource optimization.
- **Pain Points Addressed:** Inefficient tracking of asset lifecycles leading to missed renewals or unexpected failures. Wasteful spending on unused software licenses. Suboptimal utilization of cloud resources resulting in higher costs. Difficulty in planning for asset replacements and upgrades. Lack of visibility into the total cost of ownership (TCO) of IT assets.
- **Key AI Capability:** Time Series Forecasting (for predictive maintenance), Clustering, Optimization Algorithms.
- **Savings/Pros:** Reduces unnecessary spending on unused licenses and cloud resources. Proactive hardware replacement minimizes downtime and business disruption. Improves negotiation leverage with vendors through better data on usage and needs. Optimizes resource allocation for better cost efficiency. Provides a clearer picture of asset TCO for better financial planning.
- **Cons:** Requires integration with multiple data sources, which can be complex. Accuracy of predictions depends on the quality of data. Optimization of cloud resources requires continuous monitoring and adjustment. May require investment in specialized AI tools or platforms.

103. IT Infrastructure Capacity Planning & Forecasting

- **Explanation:** Ensuring IT infrastructure (servers, storage, network bandwidth) has sufficient capacity to meet current and future demands is crucial for performance and reliability. Traditional capacity planning often relies on historical trends and manual projections, which can be inaccurate. AI can improve this by analyzing historical usage data, application performance metrics, business growth forecasts (e.g., projected user growth, transaction volumes), and even external factors like seasonality. Using time-series forecasting and machine learning, AI can predict future capacity needs with greater accuracy, allowing IT to proactively plan for upgrades or cloud scaling.
- **Implementation Strategy:** Aggregate historical infrastructure utilization data (CPU, memory, storage, network), application performance metrics, and business forecasts. Utilize time-series forecasting models (ARIMA, Prophet, deep learning) to predict future

resource demands. Segment forecasts by application, service, or location. Implement alerts for potential capacity bottlenecks. Integrate with cloud auto-scaling mechanisms where applicable.

- **Pain Points Addressed:** Performance bottlenecks and outages due to insufficient capacity. Over-provisioning of infrastructure leading to wasted resources. Reactive capacity upgrades that disrupt services. Difficulty in aligning infrastructure investments with business growth. Inaccurate forecasting leading to either shortages or surpluses.
- **Key AI Capability:** Time Series Forecasting, Machine Learning (Regression).
- **Savings/Pros:** Reduces the risk of performance issues and outages due to insufficient capacity. Optimizes infrastructure spending by avoiding over-provisioning. Enables proactive capacity upgrades, minimizing disruption. Improves alignment of IT infrastructure with business needs. Provides data-driven justification for infrastructure investments.
- **Cons:** Requires access to detailed historical utilization data and accurate business forecasts. Accuracy of forecasts depends on the stability of usage patterns and the reliability of business projections. AI models require ongoing monitoring and retraining. May require investment in specialized capacity planning tools with AI capabilities.

104. Vendor Risk Assessment & Management (Financial Stability Focus)

- **Explanation:** Assessing the financial stability of critical IT vendors is crucial to avoid disruptions to services or supply chains. Traditional vendor risk assessments often rely on manual reviews of financial statements, which can be time-consuming and may not provide a complete picture. AI can automate and enhance this process by ingesting financial data from various sources (financial databases, news articles, credit rating agencies). NLP can be used to analyze news and reports for potential financial distress signals. Machine learning models can then assess the vendor's financial health and predict potential risks, allowing organizations to proactively mitigate potential issues.
- **Implementation Strategy:** Integrate with financial data providers and credit rating agencies. Utilize NLP to analyze news and financial reports for relevant information. Develop or utilize machine learning models to assess financial stability and predict risk (e.g., probability of bankruptcy, declining credit rating). Implement a workflow for reviewing and acting upon identified risks. Continuously monitor vendor financial health.
- **Pain Points Addressed:** Difficulty in thoroughly assessing the financial stability of vendors. Time-consuming and manual review of financial documents. Risk of business disruption due to vendor financial instability. Lack of proactive monitoring of vendor financial health. Challenges in making informed decisions about vendor selection and management.
- **Key AI Capability:** Natural Language Processing (NLP), Machine Learning (Classification, Prediction).
- **Savings/Pros:** Enables more comprehensive and efficient assessment of vendor financial stability. Provides early warning signs of potential vendor financial distress. Reduces the risk of business disruption due to vendor issues. Improves decision-making regarding

vendor selection and management. Allows for proactive mitigation of vendor-related risks.

- **Cons:** Access to comprehensive financial data may require subscriptions. NLP accuracy can be affected by the quality and availability of text data. Predicting financial distress is inherently complex and models may have limitations. Requires expertise in both finance and AI to build and interpret the models.

105. IT Investment Prioritization & ROI Analysis

- **Explanation:** Organizations often have more IT investment opportunities than available resources. AI can help prioritize these investments based on potential return on investment (ROI) and alignment with strategic goals. It can ingest data on project costs, projected benefits (financial and non-financial), risk assessments (potentially from 97), and strategic priorities. AI models can then calculate potential ROI, simulate different investment scenarios, and recommend a portfolio of projects that maximizes value and aligns with the organization's strategic objectives.
- **Implementation Strategy:** Gather data on project proposals, including costs, projected benefits (financial and non-financial), and associated risks. Integrate with strategic planning systems to understand organizational priorities. Utilize AI models (e.g., multi-criteria decision analysis, optimization algorithms) to calculate potential ROI and assess strategic alignment. Develop interactive dashboards to visualize different investment scenarios and their potential outcomes.
- **Pain Points Addressed:** Subjective and inconsistent prioritization of IT investments. Difficulty in quantifying the ROI of IT projects, especially non-financial benefits. Lack of alignment between IT investments and strategic goals. Overspending on projects with low returns. Challenges in making data-driven decisions about IT investments.
- **Key AI Capability:** Multi-criteria Decision Analysis, Optimization Algorithms, Scenario Planning.
- **Savings/Pros:** Leads to better allocation of IT resources to projects with higher potential ROI. Improves alignment of IT investments with strategic goals. Enables data-driven decision-making for IT investments. Increases the likelihood of successful IT projects that deliver business value. Improves transparency and accountability in IT investment decisions.
- **Cons:** Requires accurate and comprehensive data on project costs and benefits, which can be challenging to estimate. Quantifying non-financial benefits can be subjective. AI models can be complex and require expertise to develop and interpret. Strategic priorities may change, requiring adjustments to the prioritization process.

106. Dynamic Pricing Optimization for IT Services (Internal/External)

- **Explanation:** For IT organizations that charge for services (internally to business units or externally), AI can optimize pricing strategies. It can analyze factors like service consumption patterns, cost of delivery, market demand, and service level agreements

(SLAs). Machine learning models can dynamically adjust pricing to maximize revenue, optimize resource utilization, or incentivize desired behavior (e.g., shifting usage to off-peak hours). This can lead to more efficient resource allocation and better cost recovery for IT services.

- **Implementation Strategy:** Collect data on service consumption, cost of delivery (from financial systems), market pricing (if applicable), and SLA performance. Utilize machine learning models (regression, reinforcement learning) to analyze pricing elasticity and optimize pricing based on defined objectives (e.g., maximize revenue, optimize utilization). Implement dynamic pricing mechanisms within billing systems or service catalogs. Monitor the impact of pricing changes and adjust models as needed.
- **Pain Points Addressed:** Inefficient pricing models that don't reflect actual costs or demand. Difficulty in optimizing resource utilization through pricing. Lost revenue opportunities due to static pricing. Challenges in incentivizing desired service consumption patterns. Lack of data-driven insights into pricing effectiveness.
- **Key AI Capability:** Regression Analysis, Reinforcement Learning.
- **Savings/Pros:** Potential for increased revenue or better cost recovery for IT services. Improved resource utilization by incentivizing desired consumption patterns. More competitive pricing in external markets. Data-driven insights into pricing effectiveness. Ability to dynamically adjust pricing to changing conditions.
- **Cons:** Requires sophisticated data collection and analysis infrastructure. Implementing dynamic pricing can be complex and may face resistance from users. Requires careful consideration of fairness and transparency in pricing. Models need continuous monitoring and adjustment. May require specialized pricing optimization tools.

107. AI-Powered IT Service Portfolio Management

- **Explanation:** Managing a complex portfolio of IT services can be challenging. AI can help optimize this by analyzing service usage patterns, cost of delivery, business value, and alignment with strategic goals. Machine learning can identify underutilized or redundant services, predict future demand for services, and recommend opportunities for service consolidation or modernization. This helps IT organizations streamline their service offerings, reduce costs, and focus on services that provide the most business value.
- **Implementation Strategy:** Collect data on service usage (from monitoring tools), cost of delivery (from financial systems), business value (potentially from surveys or business impact analysis), and strategic alignment. Utilize machine learning techniques like clustering, association rule mining, and predictive analytics to identify patterns and insights. Develop dashboards to visualize the service portfolio and recommendations. Implement a process for reviewing and acting on AI-driven recommendations.
- **Pain Points Addressed:** Inefficient management of a large and complex service portfolio. Difficulty in identifying underutilized or redundant services. Lack of data-driven insights into service performance and value. Challenges in aligning the service portfolio with business needs. Difficulty in prioritizing investments in new or improved services.
- **Key AI Capability:** Clustering, Association Rule Mining, Predictive Analytics.

- **Savings/Pros:** Potential for cost savings by identifying and retiring underutilized or redundant services. Improved alignment of the service portfolio with business needs. Data-driven insights for making decisions about service investments. Streamlined service offerings and reduced complexity. Better resource allocation across the service portfolio.
- **Cons:** Requires comprehensive data on service usage, costs, and value. Defining and measuring business value can be challenging. AI recommendations require human review and validation. May require changes to IT processes and governance.

108. IT Skills Gap Analysis & Training Recommendation

- **Explanation:** Identifying and addressing IT skills gaps is crucial for successful digital transformation. AI can automate and enhance this process by analyzing employee skills data (from HR systems, performance reviews), project requirements, and emerging technology trends. NLP can be used to analyze job descriptions and training materials. Machine learning can identify skills gaps within the organization and recommend personalized training programs to address these gaps, ensuring the IT workforce has the necessary skills for future needs.
- **Implementation Strategy:** Integrate data from HR systems (skills inventory), project management tools (skills required for projects), and learning management systems (training history). Utilize NLP to analyze job descriptions, training content, and industry reports. Apply machine learning models to identify skills gaps and recommend relevant training programs. Develop a platform for employees to access personalized training recommendations.
- **Pain Points Addressed:** Difficulty in identifying current and future IT skills gaps. Inefficient and generic training programs. Lack of visibility into employee skills and capabilities. Challenges in aligning training with business needs. Risk of project delays or failures due to skills shortages.
- **Key AI Capability:** Natural Language Processing (NLP), Machine Learning (Classification, Recommendation Systems).
- **Savings/Pros:** More efficient and targeted training programs. Reduced time and cost associated with identifying and addressing skills gaps. Improved employee skills and capabilities. Better alignment of IT skills with business needs. Reduced risk of project delays due to skills shortages.
- **Cons:** Requires accurate and up-to-date data on employee skills and project requirements. NLP analysis can be complex and require training on IT-specific language. Recommendations need to be personalized and engaging for employees. Requires collaboration between IT, HR, and training departments.

109. AI-Assisted Benchmarking of IT Costs & Performance

- **Explanation:** Understanding how an organization's IT costs and performance compare to industry benchmarks is crucial for identifying areas for improvement. AI can automate and enhance this process by ingesting data on IT spending (across categories like infrastructure, personnel, software), performance metrics (uptime, response times, incident rates), and business outcomes from external benchmarking sources and potentially anonymized data from similar organizations. AI can then analyze this data to identify areas where the organization is overspending or underperforming relative to peers, providing data-driven insights for cost optimization and performance improvement initiatives.

- **Implementation Strategy:** Identify relevant benchmarking data sources (industry reports, analyst data, potentially anonymized peer data). Develop data integration pipelines to ingest and standardize this external data along with internal IT cost and performance data. Utilize AI techniques like clustering and anomaly detection to compare the organization's metrics against benchmarks and identify significant deviations. Visualize the benchmarking results on dashboards, highlighting areas needing attention.

- **Pain Points Addressed:** Difficulty in obtaining relevant and comparable benchmarking data. Time-consuming manual effort to analyze and compare internal data against benchmarks. Lack of objective insights into IT cost efficiency and performance relative to peers. Challenges in identifying specific areas for improvement based on benchmarking.

- **Key AI Capability:** Clustering, Anomaly Detection, Data Integration.

- **Savings/Pros:** Provides objective, data-driven insights into IT cost efficiency and performance. Identifies specific areas where the organization can reduce costs or improve performance. Facilitates better decision-making regarding IT investments and operational improvements. Enables tracking progress against industry standards. Strengthens business cases for IT initiatives based on benchmarking data.

- **Cons:** Access to high-quality and relevant benchmarking data can be expensive or limited. Ensuring data comparability across organizations can be challenging. AI analysis requires expertise in both data analysis and IT benchmarking. Benchmarks represent averages and may not be directly applicable to all organizations.

110. Scenario Planning for IT Strategy & Investments

- **Explanation:** Planning for the future of IT involves dealing with uncertainty. AI can assist in scenario planning by analyzing historical data, market trends, and potential future events to create different plausible scenarios for the IT landscape. This could include scenarios around technological advancements, economic shifts, changes in business strategy, or evolving regulatory requirements. AI models can then help evaluate the potential impact of each scenario on existing IT strategies and investments, allowing organizations to develop more resilient and adaptable plans.

- **Implementation Strategy:** Identify key drivers of change and potential future uncertainties relevant to the IT landscape. Gather data on historical trends, market forecasts, and expert opinions related to these drivers. Utilize AI techniques like simulation modeling, time-series forecasting, and sensitivity analysis to develop different plausible scenarios. Evaluate the impact of each scenario on existing IT strategies and investments. Develop contingency plans and flexible investment strategies that perform well across multiple scenarios.

- **Pain Points Addressed:** Difficulty in planning for an uncertain future. Risk of strategies and investments becoming obsolete due to unforeseen events. Lack of a structured approach to considering different possibilities. Challenges in evaluating the resilience of IT plans.
- **Key AI Capability:** Simulation Modeling, Time Series Forecasting, Sensitivity Analysis.
- **Savings/Pros:** Leads to more robust and adaptable IT strategies and investments. Reduces the risk of being caught off guard by future events. Improves decision-making by considering a range of possibilities. Facilitates the development of contingency plans. Enhances communication and alignment among stakeholders regarding future IT direction.
- **Cons:** Building accurate and meaningful scenario models can be complex and require significant data and expertise. The future is inherently uncertain, and AI models cannot predict it perfectly. Requires ongoing monitoring of the environment and updates to the scenarios. May require specialized scenario planning tools with AI capabilities.

Chapter 13: Conclusion - Charting Your AI-Powered Future

13.1 Key Themes and Takeaways

The chapters in this guide have highlighted how Artificial Intelligence can play a transformative role across every domain of hybrid cloud and data center operations, from monitoring and automation to security, cost optimization, and beyond. Key overarching lessons include:

- **Data as the Lifeblood:** Nearly all AI-driven initiatives depend on capturing, storing, and curating high-quality data (logs, metrics, usage statistics, etc.). The phrase "Garbage In, Garbage Out" repeatedly surfaced in preceding chapters, underscoring data's make-or-break influence on AI solutions.
- **Proactive vs. Reactive:** AI excels at identifying subtle patterns, anomalies, and leading indicators that humans might miss. By shifting from reactive, threshold-based alerts to more predictive analytics, IT can significantly reduce incidents, downtime, and cost.
- **Integration is Essential:** The most impactful AI outcomes appear when data from previously siloed sources (e.g., logs, network flows, cloud cost data) is analyzed holistically. This requires robust data pipelines, a well-maintained CMDB, and consistent asset tagging.
- **Automation with Safeguards:** Many use cases (e.g., self-healing infrastructure, risk-based OS patching) speak to partial or full automation. Yet, each also highlights the need for thorough testing, clear rollback strategies, and human oversight. AI-augmented automation can deliver powerful benefits, but only when carefully governed.
- **Ethical and Human Factors:** From risk-based security escalations to cost allocation, AI-driven decisions can affect individuals and budgets. Ethical considerations, transparent decision-making, and user adoption (including skill development) are all crucial to success.

13.2 Building an AI Strategy for IT Infrastructure

AI initiatives often flourish when guided by a coherent strategy rather than a scattershot approach. Key suggestions include:

1. **Align with Business Goals:** Whether reducing operational costs, improving security posture, or accelerating product releases, ensure each AI use case directly contributes to measurable outcomes that matter to stakeholders.
2. **Adopt a Layered Data Architecture:** A well-integrated data pipeline—covering ingestion, storage, enrichment, and analytics—is the foundation upon which AI thrives.

3. **Treat AI like a Product, Not a Project:** Successful AI in IT is not "one-and-done." It requires ongoing model tuning, data updates, feedback loops, and version control.
4. **Prioritize High-Value Use Cases:** Start by tackling a few, well-scoped problems that can yield quick wins and measurable ROI. Use successes to build momentum and stakeholder confidence.

13.3 Starting Small, Scaling Smart

Although the potential use cases described in this guide are numerous, realistically, most organizations should begin with a smaller set of challenges where the impact is high and feasibility is clear. For instance:

- **Predictive Hardware Failure Detection** or **Metric Anomaly Detection** can be good starting points to prove tangible ROI ().
- **Automated Incident Prioritization** and **Intelligent Log Summarization** can reduce workload for IT support teams immediately ().

Once early wins are achieved, organizations can broaden their scope to more complex AI-driven transformations, such as **AI-Driven Infrastructure Provisioning** or **Cross-Cloud/Region Workload Placement Optimization**.

13.4 The Human Element: Skills, Culture, and Ethics

A consistent theme throughout these chapters is that AI augments human expertise rather than replaces it. Critical considerations include:

- **Upskilling:** Equip teams with basic data science literacy, AI tool proficiency, and an understanding of how to interpret AI outputs.
- **Change Management:** Workflows will shift. Encourage collaboration and transparency, and communicate the "why" behind AI-driven changes.
- **Ethical Oversight:** Whether it's analyzing user data for endpoint performance or generating risk scores in security, put guardrails in place to protect privacy and mitigate bias.

13.5 The Road Ahead: Continuous Learning and Adaptation

AI capabilities are evolving at a rapid pace, as are the complexities of hybrid cloud, data center technologies, and security threats. Organizations that embrace a culture of continuous learning—running pilots, iterating, and refining—will derive the most long-term value. Key focuses for the next wave of IT AI might include:

- **Deeper Integration with DevOps:** Automated code quality analysis, predictive build/deployment failure detection, and advanced "shift-left" security scanning.

- **Extended FinOps Maturity:** Real-time cost optimization decisions, advanced forecasting, and deeper AI-driven guidance around sustainability.
- **Autonomous Infrastructure & Self-Tuning Systems:** Combining multiple AI layers—monitoring, anomaly detection, orchestration, and resolution—into ever-more self-regulating systems.

In short, organizations that treat AI as a continuous journey—rather than a single milestone—are best positioned to adapt to market changes, outpace competitors, and support evolving business demands.

Chapter 14. Contact & Feedback

We welcome continued dialogue, feedback, and real-world examples of how your organization uses AI in IT. Connect via below to share experiences, raise questions, or suggest improvements.

Email: manish@themanishkapoor.com

Website: www.xioserv.com | www.TheManishKapoor.com | www.maxxwellcooper.com

Contact: +1-7706968037